THE
MIND-BOGGLING
UNIVERSE

THE MIND-BOGGLING UNIVERSE

A Dazzling Scientific
Journey Through Distant
Space and Time

NEIL McALEER

Doubleday & Company, Inc., Garden City
New York
1987

To Arvilla Bowers
and
Ellen and Howard Nimick

Library of Congress Cataloging-in-Publication Data

McAleer, Neil, 1942–
    The mind-boggling universe.

    Includes index.
    1. Astronomy—Popular works. 2. Cosmology—Popular works. I. Title.
QB44.2.M425   1987   523   86-2183
ISBN 0-385-23040-0
ISBN 0-385-23039-7 (pbk.)

CONTENTS

PREFACE

When the Universe was trillions of times less than 1 trillionth of a second old, good science tells us, it was smaller than a grain of sand, the point of a needle, or the smallest cells in your body. Much, much smaller. Do you believe this? It's impossible, isn't it? Nothing in human existence prepares us for such a concept, neither trees from acorns nor people from sex cells. Nothing ever will. The mind boggles.

But this is an aspect of the Big Bang theory of the Universe. We live in an expanding Universe; this is observational fact: the galaxies and quasars are flying away from us at tremendous speeds, some at more than 90 percent the speed of light. Put the Universe on fast rewind, and science can describe the beginning: the Big Bang. Other scientific discoveries, especially that of the all-pervasive microwave background radiation, are part of the mounting scientific evidence that the Big Bang actually occurred some 15 billion years ago. Most scientists today believe that this is how our Universe was born; only the first few trillion-trillionths of a second are in serious doubt, in the unpredictable realm of quantum physics, where even Einstein's General Theory of Relativity does not apply.

And what of the future of the Universe? Will it expand forever? Will it collapse and return to nothingness? Will a new universe be created? The Hubble Space Telescope will soon be gathering the observational data to help scientists find the real answer. Scientific theory offers several scenarios. The one based on the inflation model of the Big Bang describes a Universe that will expand forever, its expansion always slowing. Eventually all stars will die, all black holes will evaporate, and all atoms but one kind will decay. What will these last atoms be in this far future Universe, when 1 trillion years equals a cosmic instant? They will be positronium atoms, composed of an electron and its antimatter positron. But the most amazing thing about these last atoms of the Universe will be their size, which science can project by putting the expansion of the Universe and nuclear physics on fast forward. Their size will be, serious scientists tell us, 1 billion times larger than the entire visible Universe of today! Again, the cosmic boggle!

Modern astronomy is filled with cosmic amazements, and new ones are found every year. The mysterious quasars, distant and small objects that are often 5 trillion times as bright as our Sun, are probably the violent centers of early galaxies. In their centers there may be black holes with masses as great as 10 billion Suns. Our own Milky Way's center is believed to contain a black hole. And astronomers are discovering supergalaxies, with masses equal to 3 trillion Suns, and great strings of galaxies, the largest known organized structures in the Universe, that may extend 1 billion light-years or more—a good portion of the observable Universe.

Much closer to home, and with much more concrete evidence from chemistry and nuclear physics to prove it, science also tells us that each and every one of us is created from the stuff of dead stars. What? Yes. Life depends on heavy elements (the calcium of our bones, the carbon of our flesh, the iron of our blood) but there were no heavy elements in the early Universe—just the pristine and light elements hydrogen and helium. The heavy elements essential for the creation of planets and living things were fused in the centers of the first few generations of large stars. When these stars burned out and exploded, the star stuff with its heavier elements was hurled into interstellar space. Over tens of millions of years, great clouds of gas and dust formed and condensed, and new stars were born.

One of these billions of new cosmic condensations was our Sun and its planets. Life was made possible against tremendous odds, but we are here on planet Earth, having been sculptured out of elemental star stuff. So has this book been created out of primordial star stuff. Enjoy it. And don't forget to sometimes get away from the city lights and see with your own eyes the ancient light from distant galaxies that has been traveling through space and time for millions of years. Such meditation under clear, moonless, night skies will stir the same wonder that early humans felt millions of years ago.

Any book about astronomy and the Universe owes a large debt to the community of thousands of professional astronomers who design their intricate research projects, carry them out, and then interpret what are often billions of data bits against the rich legacy of their profession. The discoveries and theories of these men and women in the twentieth century have taken us to the beginning of our Universe, out in space and time to cosmic wonders that no longer exist except for their light radiating across the light-years. And in the years to come, these same dedicated professionals, who so often schedule their lives around the motions of the stars, may come to know if other life exists in our galaxy and also how our Universe will end, trillions of years from now.

I want to thank T. A. Heppenheimer of the Center for Space Science and Robert R. Young of Science Communicators, Inc., for their research assistance on this project. Special thanks also go to my editor, Nicholas Bakalar, who has always been helpful, encouraging, and patient; and to his assistant, Rachel Klayman.

For assistance in obtaining photographs, I want to thank the professional astronomers who kindly gave photographs of their work and whose names appear in the photo credit lines; and also Rhea Goodwin, Mount Wilson and Las Campanas Observatories; David F. Malin, Anglo-Australian Telescope; Ann Palfreyman, Palomar Observatory; Agnes Paulsen, National Optical Astronomy Observatories; Arlene Walsh, Smithsonian Institution Astrophysical Observatory; and Diane Moss, American Institute of Physics.

The fire is in [the stars] whereof we are born:
The music of their motion may be ours.

George Meredith—"Meditation Under Stars"

The universe is full of matter and force. Yet in all that force—among the bulks and gravities, the rain of cosmic light, the bombardments of energy—how little spirit! How small are these decimal points of intelligence.

Ray Bradbury—*Why Man Explores*

CHAPTER 1

OUR MILKY WAY HOME

The Galaxy, that Milky Way . . .
Powdered with Stars.

—John Milton, *Paradise Lost*

Our Yellow Galaxy from Afar

If human eyes could view our great spiral Milky Way Galaxy from afar—from at least 300,000 light-years (three galactic diameters)—and a predominant blended color emerged from the billions of white, blue, yellow, green, orange, and red stars, our galaxy would appear slightly yellow in its central regions, with a hazy luminosity surrounding it. The spiral arms would be quite inconspicuous—no more than a faint brightening against the sky of our intergalactic planet.

The Galaxy from Earth

Our home galaxy, an immense pinwheel of billions of stars, is best seen on a clear, moonless night, in late summer or early fall, away from the bright lights of towns and cities. One needs neither telescope nor binoculars to see many of the Galaxy's most important features. From the dark rural skies of a state or national park, it can be seen in all its shimmering beauty: the great star clouds of the hub, the hazy glow of the myriad of clusters and gaseous nebulae of the arms, and the dark path of obscuring dust called the Great Rift. Although binoculars are probably the best optical instrument to view the Milky Way, the main features can be seen with the unaided human eye.

Unless a person is able to leave the light pollution behind, the most spectacular views will come after midnight, when traffic and lights interfere least. Then, in the hours before dawn, the atmosphere is most steady, without heat currents, and transparent.

Good views of the Galaxy from North America and Europe are possible as soon as twilight fades. Starting at the northern horizon near the first-magnitude star Capella in late summer, the faintly glowing band of the great disk of stars sweeps up through the constellation Perseus and the "W" of Cassiopeia to Cygnus' "northern cross," almost overhead. It is here that binoculars or a small telescope will reveal the richness of stars, which first suggested to Galileo Galilei in 1609 and 1610 the true nature of that band of light.

"I have observed the nature and material of the Milky Way," he wrote. "With the aid of the telescope this has been scrutinized so directly and with such ocular certainty that all the disputes which have vexed philosophers through so many ages have been resolved. . . . The Galaxy is, in fact, nothing but . . . innumerable stars grouped together in clusters. . . ." Thus ended one of the great mysteries of the nighttime sky. Galileo believed the controversy had ended. Actually, it was just beginning and would continue to rage for another three centuries.

Overhead, in Cygnus the Swan, the softly glowing river of stars divides into two streams around the Great Rift, caused by intervening dust in the plane of the Galaxy. The Rift is skirted by the bright stars of the Summer Triangle: Deneb, at the Swan's tail; Vega, in Lyra, the Harp; and Altair, in Aquila, the Eagle. It continues south, obscuring the galactic center in Sagittarius, at the southern horizon.

On clear, haze-free nights at exceptionally dark-sky locations, the center, in Sagittarius, can be mistaken for a cloud, hanging motionless and bright in the southern sky. In the very darkest locations, the beauty of the galactic disk seems just below the threshold of vision. The eye glimpses the black sky mottled with a soft marbled glow just between the stars.

Sharks, Turtles, and the Celestial River

While human eyes have stretched to see the glimmering band of our home galaxy, human minds have extended their reach to explain it.

The early Arabs called it *Al Nahr*, the river. To the Hebrews it was *N_e har di Nur*, the river of light. In eleventh-century Sanskrit it was known as the Bed of the Ganges. Chinese and Japanese saw *Tien Ho*, the celestial river, a silver river whose schools of fish were frightened away from the crescent Moon's hook. The starry fish could be seen only in dark skies, when the Moon was down.

The Polynesian islanders saw it as the great, blue, cloud-eating shark, and in North America the Ottawa Indians saw a muddy river stirred by the passage of a celestial turtle.

Some people in the ancient world guessed at its true nature and a few myths came close, but the Milky Way was slow to reveal its secrets. Only in the past twenty-five years have many of the missing puzzle pieces been found, although we have known the basics of its nature for some time.

The Greeks and others saw the Galaxy. Romans called it *Via Lactis* or *Via Lactea,* the milky way. The Midland Dutch knew it as *Vronelden Straet*, the women's way, and in the north, in East Friesland, it was the *Melkpath*, the milk path. *Linnunrata*, the birds' way, is the Finnish name. Ancient Anglo-Saxons called it *Waetlinga Straet*, the path of the Waetlings (giant sons of King Waetla), and the Vikings knew it as *Wuotanes Weg*, the path of their chief god, Odin.

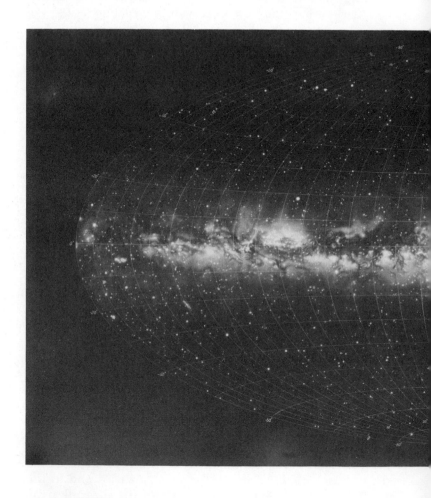

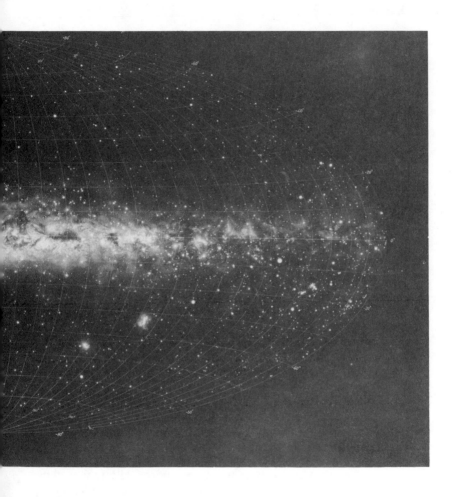

Panorama of the Milky Way Galaxy as seen from Earth. This composite painting was made from many wide-angle photographs. *Courtesy Lund Observatory.*

Perhaps the most illustrative of all is the Swedish "winter street," describing its striking arch across a clear, glittering December sky.

Before the Sun

Imagine a time machine in which we could zoom forward to the death of the Sun or flash back to a time when the Sun was not yet born, say 10 billion years ago. What would our galaxy have looked like those billions of years ago?

For one thing, it would be brilliant. The birth of millions of stars would be underway. Spectacularly brilliant large, hot stars, whose lives might span only a million years, would be forming from dark clouds of interstellar matter. Their luminosity would be dazzling to any extraterrestrial beings alive at that remote time, if they had eyes to see.

One estimate is that the brightness of the Galaxy might have been a hundred times greater than it is today. The Milky Way is now about as bright as 10 billion Suns. The early Galaxy might have given off light equal to 1 trillion (1 thousand billion) Suns.

Even though our own star and its system, including the planet Earth, had not yet formed, and no one was there to see, we can imagine the Milky Way's appearance using a brief calculation.

In the high southern sky on spring evenings is the first-magnitude star Regulus in the constellation Leo, the Lion. It is about a hundred times brighter than the dimmest, sixth-magnitude star we can see with our unaided eye on a dark night. Imagine what the Milky Way would look like if more than a thousand of the dimmest stars, just visible to our eyes now, were as bright as Regulus. Even more striking would be the dimmer stars that compose the unresolved soft, white glow of our galaxy. These would sparkle like thousands of second-, third-, and fourth-magnitude objects, with tens of thousands of dim stars visible to us in the darkest sky instead of the two thousand or so we can now see.

Another striking feature would be the sky's color. When we look at the night sky we see color only in the very brightest stars, because of our eyes' limits. Most stars appear as dim, white objects, although in a telescope many have color because of the light-gathering power of the instrument. The early Milky Way would have thousands of brightly colored stars, many glowing blue-hot during their short lifetimes. A celestial kaleidoscope.

With the Milky Way so dazzling, we probably would be able to see the great clouds and globs of dark matter silhouetted against the glow, giving true three-dimensional depth to the sky. What a view it would have been! Not even streetlights or neon signs would have interfered.

The Great Displacers

Nicolaus Copernicus displaced the Earth as the center of the Universe in the sixteenth century and put the Sun in its place. Harlow Shapley, an American astronomer, displaced the Sun and Solar System from the center of the Universe in the early-twentieth century by determining the general size and shape of the Galaxy. He did this by measuring the distances to the globular star clusters, aided by the guiding lights of the Cepheid variable stars within these clusters, whose pulsing light became the units on a new type of cosmic ruler.

After two years of work with the 60-inch telescope at Mount Wilson Observatory, Shapley realized that the globular clusters, great spherical conglomerates of stars, were all concentrated in a sphere in one area of the sky: in the direction of Sagittarius. Their positions indicated that the center of the Galaxy was nowhere near our solar system and that the Sun was out in the galactic suburbs. While Shapley's initial estimates of the Galaxy's dimensions were too high because of the effects of interstellar gas and dust on distant starlight, he calculated the correct dimension (still used today) by 1930. Shapley's pioneering work once and for all put the Sun

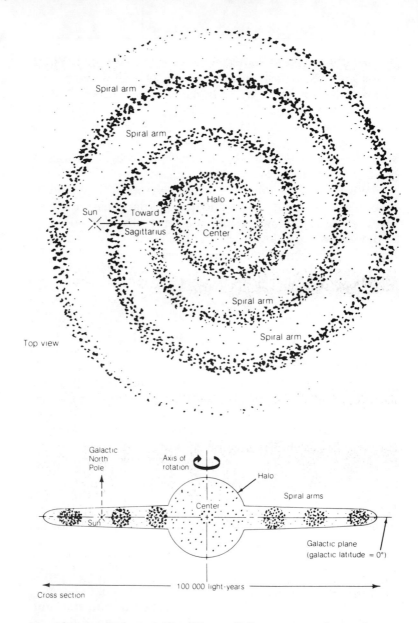

Two diagrams of our Milky Way—a full-on view and an edge-on view, showing the position of our Sun and Solar System some 30,000 light-years from the center. *Courtesy NASA.*

The Sagittarius region of our galaxy, showing a portion of the dark path of obscuring dust called the Great Rift, which hides the mysterious center. A Palomar Observatory Photograph. *Courtesy California Institute of Technology.*

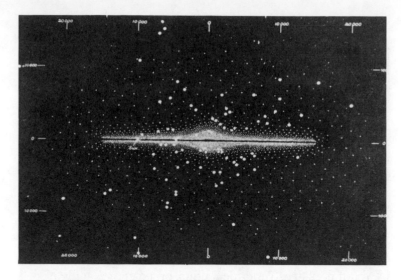

Edge-on diagram of the Galaxy, showing position of the globular clusters that define its dimensions. There are about 125 globular clusters moving in giant elliptical orbits around the galactic core. *Courtesy The American Institute of Physics.*

in its rightful place: about 30,000 light-years out from the Galaxy's center. If the diameter of our solar system were represented by 1 inch (2.54 centimeters), the center of the Galaxy would be about 379 miles (609 kilometers) away.

Astronomical Distances

Astronomers use a number of special measuring units because of the immensity of their subject. Their use makes descriptions more concise, and difficult calculations easier. In this book, these units will sometimes be used interchangeably. At other times, more than one measurement will be used (such as miles and kilometers) to aid the reader. Here are the most important astronomical measurements:

Astronomical unit (AU). The mean distance between the Sun and the Earth, roughly 93 million miles

(149,600,000 kilometers × 1.609 = 92,529,000 miles). Referred to by astronomers as the AU, the unit is used to measure distances within the Solar System or between nearby close pairs of stars. One astronomical unit also equals 499 light-seconds (8 minutes and somewhat over 19 seconds)—the time it takes light to travel from the Sun to the Earth. Walking at a brisk pace (3 miles, or 5 kilometers, per hour, it would take a person more than 3,500 years to hike a distance equal to an astronomical unit.

Light-year. The distance that light, or any electromagnetic radiation, travels in 1 year in a vacuum. Hence, a year is also the *time* it takes for light or other radiation to cross the distance of a light-year. This is about 63,240 astronomical units, or a distance sufficient to line up 800 Solar Systems side by side. The speed of light is about 6 trillion miles per year, or 299,793 kilometers per second. If you were to hop into your car and travel at the speed limit of 55 miles per hour (88 kilometers per hour), it would take you 12.2 million years to travel 1 light-year. The Sun would be long dead before you had gone this far . . . and of course so would you.

Parsec. Astronomers use this unit to measure distances beyond our solar system. It is sometimes used instead of light-years for great distances. One parsec equals 3.26 light-years. Parsec is an abbreviation for parallax-second, or the distance at which an object would seem to change its position by 1 second of arc when viewed from opposite sides of the Earth's orbit, 6 months apart. A second of arc, by the way, is only one 1,800th the Moon's diameter, or one 3,600th the width of your little finger held at arm's length. Observing something against a background from two positions is called observing its parallax.

Kiloparsec. Using the standard prefixes of the metric system, 1,000 parsecs becomes 1 kiloparsec. Distances across our Milky Way Galaxy are often given in kiloparsecs. This is, of course, 3,260 light-years. Our Sun is about 8.5 kiloparsecs from the Milky Way's center.

Megaparsec. Distances to other galaxies are usually measured in megaparsecs, each of which equals 1 million parsecs. These numbers are usually rounded off because of the large uncertainties at these great distances. If the edge of the expanding Universe is 18 billion light-years (5.52 billion parsecs; 5.52 thousand megaparsecs) away, which some astronomers calculate, then the Big Bang would have occurred 18 billion years ago.

The Birth of the Milky Way

From the Big Bang came the pristine elements, hydrogen and helium, from which our galaxy was created. Probably some kind of density variations during the early expanding Universe were amplified over time, once matter became dominant over radiation, and caused the condensation of our protogalactic cloud about 12 billion years ago. The great, primordial cloud was composed of 75 percent hydrogen and 25 percent helium. No heavier elements existed at this time, nor did any stars. Life was impossible, because it depends on second-generation stars that contain the heavier elements, forged in their fusion furnaces.

Scientists believe our massive protogalaxy was initially in the shape of a great sphere that was rotating. The protocloud began gravitational collapse, and when it collapsed to a diameter of about 100,000 light-years, its increasing density caused internal condensations to appear. The great globular star clusters, still existing today, were born from these smaller condensations. They are the oldest objects in our galaxy, still defining the primordial spherical shape of the protogalactic cloud.

Gravitational collapse continued, leaving the globular clusters behind, and the denser, rotating inner cloud formed into a disk. About 1 billion years later, after several revolutions, the spiral arms emerged in the disk, where dense gas

A globular cluster in Canes Venatici that contains about 1 million stars. One of the oldest and brightest, this globular cluster was one of those studied by Harlow Shapley to help determine the size and shape of our galaxy. A Palomar Observatory Photograph. *Courtesy California Institute of Technology.*

Positions of globular clusters are identified by circles in this photograph in Sagittarius toward the center of the Galaxy. *Courtesy Yerkes Observatory.*

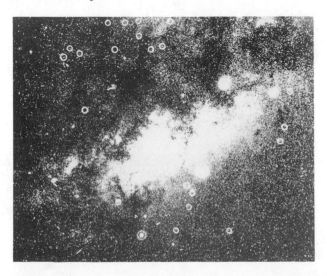

clouds contracted even further, and clusters of stars were spawned. Many of these original stars burned rapidly and died in convulsive explosions, supernovae, after just a few million years, spewing forth their star stuff. Their demise created new, enriched interstellar clouds that contained the first heavy elements, forged in their stellar interiors. From this debris came a second generation of stars. The Sun was among them, and its birth, along with the planets, had much in common with the Galaxy's, but on a much smaller scale. A protosolar cloud condensed and gravitationally collapsed, forming a rotating disk of gaseous material that would become the Earth and other planets.

The elapsed time from protogalaxy to Solar System was about 7.5 billion years; from Solar System to the first microscopic life on Earth, about 1 billion years; from microscopic life to us, about 3.5 billion years. Add it all up and what have you got? About 12 billion years. If these 12 billion years were compressed into 1 year, then humankind appeared on planet Earth about 1 hour, 45 minutes ago, and Galileo Galilei made his telescope discoveries about 1 second ago.

A Sun's Pace

The Sun moves at a speed of about 633,000 miles (1,018,000 kilometers) per hour around our galaxy and draws the retinue of planets, including Earth, with it. The Sun wobbles slightly, moving from side to side as it progresses along its path. This is not the reason, however, that some people feel wobbly in the morning.

Follow the Sun

Besides making its long voyage around the Galaxy every 225 million years or so, the Sun also takes shorter excursions around the local stellar neighborhood. Sir William Herschel was the first to discover that the Sun and the entire Solar

System were heading in the direction of the constellation Hercules. He did this in 1783 by realizing that stars were moving apart in this direction and moving together in the opposite direction. Later refinements put the "Apex of the Sun's Way" at a point in space not far from the star Vega, which is 27 light-years away.

The Sun is traveling toward this point at 45,000 miles (72,000 kilometers) per hour. Assuming that the Sun and Solar System are heading directly at Vega, and assuming Vega's motion is not drastically changed, there could be a cataclysmic collision between the Sun and Vega in about 450,000 years—probably enough time for humankind to build economical starships for a getaway.

Starship *Magellan*

The distance around the Galaxy's disk, the greatly flattened and thin spiral that surrounds the dense bulge (nucleus) at the center, measures about 1.85 million trillion miles, or 2.99 million trillion kilometers, which amounts to over 300,000 light-years. Even traveling at 25 percent the speed of light (167 million miles per hour, 269 million kilometers per hour), a starship of the future, the *Magellan*, would still take 1.25 million years to circumnavigate the galactic disk. The Earth, at its present orbital speed around the Sun, would take about 5.6 million times longer, or about 7 trillion years.

The Scenic Spiral Route

Our galaxy's longest spiral arm may wind around three times and has a total length of about 125,000 light-years. If a superhighway were built along this arm, it would take a car about 1.5 trillion years at 55 miles (88 kilometers) per hour to cover the route—some seventy-five times the theoretical age of the Universe. Going over the speed limit would not help matters much.

Changing Arms

If we could observe our galaxy from a distance of 300,000 light-years—a distance equal to about three galactic diameters—and view it in cosmic time-lapse motion, with each million years of time compressed into 1 minute, then the Sun's rotation around the galactic center would take 3 hours, 50 minutes (from the real 230 million years). The spiral-arm pattern, however, would take more than twice that long to make a complete revolution around the center, about 8 hours of this compressed cosmic time (from the real 480 million years), because the Galaxy's density-wave pattern, which gives the spiral arms their shape, has its own speed, completely independent of the star system and gas and dust that it attracts gravitationally but which move through it at greater speeds. Like the ocean, the Galaxy has waves, and like the ocean waves, which are continuously formed by ever-different water, so the density waves of the Galaxy are formed by ever-different stars and star stuff.

From our distant observation post, we would track the Sun for one revolution and find it in unfamiliar territory— somewhere in the spiral arms that are now hidden from our optical and radio view on the far side of the Galaxy.

Losing Sight of the Galaxy's Light

The brightness of the Milky Way Galaxy equals about 10 billion suns. Its luminous spiral would appear as bright as Venus from 59,000 light-years away. The human eye would lose sight of it at a distance of 6.5 million light-years—about three times the distance to the Andromeda Galaxy.

The Great Rift

Starlight from billions of stars in the direction of our galaxy's center is absorbed and blocked off by the Great Rift

—a vast belt of dark dust and gas clouds that runs from the constellation Cygnus to Sagittarius and divides the Milky Way (at visual wavelengths, at least) into two parallel star streams that arch all the way from the stars Vega and Altair to the southern horizon. Most of the obscuring clouds of the Great Rift are 4,000 to 5,000 light-years away and prevent optical observations of our galaxy's center. It amounts to a great dust lane that surrounds the galactic equator, similar to those seen in other spiral galaxies viewed from afar, such as the galaxies NGC 891 and NGC 4565.

The dark clouds of the Great Rift, as well as the other gas and dust between it and our Solar System, allow only one ten-billionth of the light from the Galaxy's brilliant core to reach our local galactic neighborhood. If we received one ten-billionth of the light from the Sun that we do, the Earth's temperature would fall to −272 degrees Celsius (−458 degrees Fahrenheit), and the only life that could survive would be a few spores.

From Sagittarius to Cassiopeia, this mosaic of the Milky Way shows a part of the Great Rift, which prevents optical view of our galaxy's center and perhaps its immense black hole. A Palomar Observatory Photograph. *Courtesy California Institute of Technology.*

This view of spiral galaxy NGC 891 depicts what the Milky Way's Great Rift of dust and gas would look like from afar. *Courtesy Mount Wilson and Las Campanas Observatories of the Carnegie Institution of Washington.*

Counting the Grains

There are a great many more dust grains in the Galaxy than there are grains of sand on Earth. The Galaxy contains *more* than

100,000,000,000,000,000,000,000,000,000,000,000,000,-
000,000,000,000,000

or 100 thousand trillion trillion trillion trillion (10^{53}) dust grains.

How many more? At least twice as many.

The Old Discovery

All our knowledge about the center of our galaxy has been learned in the past decade, with revolutionary advances in infrared and radio astronomy, and all the information about the congested stars, the powerful radiation, the swirling gas and dust, the possible black hole of the nucleus— is almost 30,000 years old, the time it takes the radiation to reach Earth.

The Dim Center

The Galaxy's center is forever hidden from the view of optical telescopes because of the intervening thick clouds of dust and gas. Thanks to infrared and X-ray astronomy, however, our knowledge about the mysterious center is growing.

How much is the light from the galactic center dimmed before it reaches Earth? As it travels across the 30,000 light-years, the light becomes 10 billion times dimmer than when it began.

The Local Big Bang

Radio astronomers discovered two gigantic arms of hydrogen gas in the 1960s that are expanding outward from the galactic center. The sunwardside hydrogen arm, located between us and the center, is about 10,000 light-years out from the galactic nucleus (one third the distance to the Sun), moving toward us at about 112,000 miles (180,000 kilometers) per hour. Its mass is estimated to be equal to about 10 million Suns, and it is rotating around the galactic center, as well as expanding outward, at 470,000 miles (756,000 kilometers) per hour.

On the other side of our galaxy, the second hydrogen arm is rushing out at an even greater velocity: over 300,000 miles (483,000 kilometers) per hour. Together, both arms suggest a ring structure. Large amounts of the expanding hydrogen gas have also been detected above and below the plane of the galactic disk, and at dead center of this vast hydrogen expansion is Sagittarius A, the most powerful radio source yet detected, but extremely small on a galactic scale— only 40 light-years in diameter. Its energy output, relative to its size, makes it comparable to the enigmatic quasars (see Chapter 4, "Quasars and Company").

What began all this gaseous commotion? Probably a tremendous explosion at the center of the Galaxy some 10–12 million years ago, when the nucleus blasted away 100 million Suns' worth of matter. The stupendous energy of this event has been estimated at a thousand times the total 10-billion-year, life-span, energy of the Sun.

The X-Ray Ridge

In the mid-1980s, the space-based *Exosat* X-ray observatory, which can peer through the thick clouds of stars, gas, and dust that block out the center of the Galaxy to optical astronomy, discovered an unusual "ridge" of X-ray emissions. British astronomers report that the ridge stretches 80 degrees across the galactic center and that it is only 2 degrees thick (4 times the diameter of the Moon) at its edges and thickens at its center to a size in the sky equal to the Big Dipper's bowl. What causes this X-ray ridge? The experts' guess is that there are either a large number of very small objects that cannot be resolved with today's equipment or immense clouds of hot ionized gas (gas with a positive electrical charge because its electrons have been stripped away).

Ring Around the Nucleus

Closer still to the galactic core than the giant expanding arms of hydrogen, about 3,000 light-years away from dead center, is a ring of molecular clouds that completely surrounds the nucleus. Associated with these molecular clouds are many gaseous nebulae, similar to the beautiful ones in the vicinity of the Sun such as the Orion nebula. This gaseous ring is expanding at about 90,000 miles (145,000 kilometers) per hour, as well as rotating around the galactic nucleus like all other galactic matter—including us. Its expansion, like that of the great hydrogen arms, is believed to be the result of a violent cataclysm in the Galaxy's center some 10 million years ago.

The molecules of the gaseous clouds emit microwaves, and this has permitted astronomers to identify many chemicals in the great molecular clouds of the ring. The large and famous cloud Sagittarius B-2, which contains enough gas and dust to equal more than 1 million Suns, has provided an extraterrestrial chemical gold mine for radio astronomers. Many of the more than fifty chemicals discovered have been found in this vast ring cloud around the Galaxy's nucleus, and bigger things, or beings, are no doubt yet to come.

The Central Power

The total infrared power emitted from the central 978 light-years of the Galaxy (less than one hundredth the galactic diameter), amounts to 1 billion times the luminosity of the Sun. If converted to thrust power, just 7 hours' worth of this energy could accelerate the entire solar system out of the Galaxy at 224,000 miles (360,000 kilometers) per hour.

The Galaxy's Heart

The mass of the Galaxy's central 3.26 light-years (equal in diameter to 2,600 solar systems) may be as much as 8 million times the mass of the Sun, which is *the* single star in an equal amount of space. Only about 2 million solar masses of this total, however, is composed of stars. What makes up

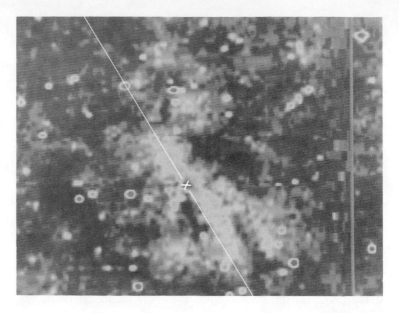

The center of the Galaxy, hidden from optical telescopes by dark clouds of dust and gas, is seen in this infrared-wavelength view. Many astronomers believe there is an immense black hole at the center—"X" marks the spot. *Courtesy Eric E. Becklin and Gerry Neugebauer, California Institute of Technology and Palomar Observatory.*

the difference? Many astronomers believe it is a massive black hole at the very heart of our galaxy, always growing larger as it constantly accretes the hot matter swirling into it.

The Galactic Weather Forecast

Coastal (hot, muggy, and calm)

The offshore currents of the galactic halo (the Galaxy's outer regions) are extremely hot, 100,000 degrees Celsius (180,000 degrees Fahrenheit), normal for the season. Extending outward from the sparsely populated halo region for some 50,000 light-years, these gas currents bring oxygen, sulfur, iron, silicon, and carbon with them.

The rest of the halo region will experience normal

amounts of condensation in and around the globular star clusters, but it will remain mostly calm and clear.

Mid-Galactic (foggy and cloudy, with possible showers)

Cloudy today in the galactic disk, with large, cool hydrogen clouds distributed throughout the region. The clouds are even more prevalent in the disk's coastal areas, and tides are high because of the effects of the Magellanic star clouds. Occasional star showers are expected to develop in the spiral arms of the galactic disk region. The thicker clouds, heated by hot new stars, will reach 10,000 degrees Celsius (18,000 degrees Fahrenheit) today. Scattered dark dust clouds will create patches of fog and limit visibility to about 6,000 light-years.

Central Galactic (hurricane warning)

A tropical-storm pattern has developed in the galactic core, with extremely high stellar winds because of the dense star concentrations. Low pressure readings indicate a powerful hurricane. At the periphery of the storm is a ring of giant hot hydrogen clouds. Even more turbulent swirling occurs deep inside these clouds around the storm's center. Weather satellites indicate that the eye of the storm is a black hole. Authorities urge evacuation of the central region.

Today's galactic weather will continue for another few billion years. Get out and enjoy it while you can.

The Growing Galaxy

Not too many years ago the Milky Way was thought to be about 100,000 light-years across and to contain some 100 billion stars. In recent years its mass has been increasing by leaps and bounds as further observations suggest that the Galaxy is much larger than previously thought—perhaps 326,000 light-years (100,000 parsecs) in diameter. This faint outer halo also is thought to contain many dim stars and very little gas and dust. Estimates now place the mass of the Milky Way at a very conservative 800 billion solar masses, with some estimates going as high as 2 trillion (2,000 billion) solar masses.

If the average star in the Milky Way is about half the Sun's size and if the larger estimates are accepted, there could be almost a thousand stars in our galaxy for each man, woman, and child on planet Earth.

Death of the Milky Way

The fate of our galaxy will depend, naturally, on the fate of the Universe. If the Universe expands forever, all the billions of stars of the Milky Way Galaxy will eventually burn out, leaving a galactic morgue of stellar corpses: dead neutron stars, dwarf stars, and black holes. The last ancient red star in the Galaxy may die in a few trillion years, leaving a dark ghost galaxy that will expand forever outward.

If the Universe halts its expansion and collapses, the Galaxy will fall through space toward all the other estimated 100 billion galaxies. As contraction continues over the aeons, the billions of galaxies will collide, and their stars, gas, and dust will eventually dissolve into a hot cosmic soup of the two basic elements—hydrogen and helium—with which the Universe began. Beyond that, there could be the ultimate black hole. Either way, the Galaxy as we know it will never exist again. The nourishing milk the ancients saw—the countless stars that life depends on—will spoil.

THE GALAXY'S STARS

Stars of the Show

Stars are the principal active objects in the Universe. Their quiet, almost imperceptible births, often steady lives, and sometimes violent deaths provide the driving force for the Universe we know, including our Milky Way Galaxy.

What are stars? They are burning spheres of hot gas which generate their own heat and light. Gravitational collapse and outward pressure create a balancing act throughout the lives of most stars. The pressure comes from heat due to contraction and later the process known as nuclear fusion. Each star has its own individual life span that is determined by its mass, so the duration of its balancing act is a result of the amount of matter that is present at its birth. And the mass of a star also determines how it will die: quietly, violently, or somewhere in between. After a star dies, its remains, rich in elements heavier than the primordial hydrogen and helium, fertilize the interstellar fields between the living stars and provide the material for future stellar generations and life.

The Average Star's Energy

The estimated amount of energy produced by a star like our Sun is more than 53 million watts each second for a square yard of its surface (64 million watts per square meter per second). This would keep more than 713,000 75-watt light bulbs burning, enough to light 100,000 average homes. All this power from a square area only half the size of a single-bed mattress; this is why fusion research is on the priority list for future energy sources.

Star Fusion

Stars burn for millions and often billions of years, and the process by which they burn is nuclear fusion. When the contraction of dust and gas raises the temperature of the proto-star's core to 10 million degrees Celsius (18 million degrees Fahrenheit), the nuclei of atoms are fused and a thermonuclear reaction is underway—a star is born. Two light nuclei of hydrogen are fused in the thermonuclear reaction and form a single heavier nucleus of helium. When the hydrogen is converted into helium, a small amount of the hydrogen's mass is converted to a tremendous amount of energy.

This conversion of matter into energy was described by Albert Einstein in his famous equation $E = mc^2$: the amount of energy produced equals the amount of mass converted times the speed of light squared. A small amount of mass, in other words, can become a great amount of energy. Through the fusion reactions occurring in the cores of stars such as our Sun, 1 pound (455 grams) of hydrogen is converted into enough energy to keep a 100-watt light bulb burning 450,000 years. The Sun converts about 660 million tons of its matter into energy each second, and has been doing this for about 5 billion years.

The Dim Dwarf Majority

Our Sun, it is often said, is an average dwarf star, slightly less bright than the average visible star in the sky. This is true enough for stars visible with the naked eye, but when telescopes are used to bring forth the light of dim stars, everything changes.

The value of the Sun's absolute visual magnitude (the brightness of the Sun as measured from a distance of 32.6 light-years) is 4.85. When the brightness of the fifty-five closest known stars is measured by that same distance standard, fifty-one of them are found to be dimmer than our Sun. The four exceptions are: Alpha Centauri A (about the same brightness, at 4.37); Sirius A (brighter, at 1.42); Procyon A (brighter, at 2.64); and Altair (brighter, at 2.24). It appears that dim dwarf stars far outnumber all other kinds of stars in the present-day Universe, but most of them will never be seen from Earth.

Counting the Stars

A great census of stars was completed in the late 1930s and showed more than 40 million visible stars in the Galaxy. But most astronomers have stopped counting, because they want to focus on individual stars and understand their life cycles and their relationships to other types of stars. Counting stars, in other words, is less important than understanding stars.

The Palomar Sky Survey, financed by the National Geographic Society, is the most extensive star atlas ever pre-

Astronomers are no longer counting stars. From now on, the count-less billions of stars can only be estimated. This region of stars is in Sagittarius. A Lick Observatory Photograph. *Courtesy Lick Observatory.*

pared. It consists of 935 pairs of photographic plates made in blue and red light. The total number of stars shown in this survey has never been counted.

The Palomar Sky Survey does not yet include the entire southern sky and goes only to the 21st magnitude. The limit of Earth-based telescopes is now about 24 magnitudes. Each increase in magnitude means that stars are seen which are 2.5 times dimmer. Earth-based telescopes today can therefore see about fifteen times as many stars as are in the survey, stars that are about fifteen times dimmer than those appearing on the Palomar plates.

Astronomy today is beyond counting stars; from now on, the countless stars can only be estimated.

A Star-Observing Feat

Astronomer R. H. Tucker and a staff of ten at the Lick Observatory accumulated 87,000 observations of stellar positions in two years (1910–11) from an observatory in San Luis, Argentina. This record feat in intensive observing has not been surpassed, and the data became part of the General Catalogue of star positions and proper motions, which was completed in 1937—a thirty-year project that required the continuous efforts of twenty people.

The Printed Stars

A three-volume atlas by Czechoslovakian Antonin Becvar is the ultimate published guide to celestial geography for small telescopes. There are eighty maps all together in Atlas Borealis (northern sky), Atlas Eclipticalis (equatorial sky), and Atlas Australis (southern sky), in which some 320,000 stars are plotted and depicted in six colors to represent spectral type. Spread out, these maps would cover almost 150 square feet (14 square meters), and it would take almost 900 continuous hours, or 112 working nights, to observe them all through a telescope if each star were allotted a modest 10 seconds.

MEASURING IMMENSITIES

Accuracy in astronomy is extremely relative. Even distances in our own solar system are constantly being refined as interplanetary spacecraft and satellites send their data back to Earth. Generally, it is safe to say that the lesser distances are more accurate than the greater distances. This will continue to hold true even as the techniques for measuring cosmic distances improve.

Star Mileages

How do we know the distance to a nearby star? We use the same method used by land surveyors, triangulation from two points, to establish the location of the star. This is called *trigonometric parallax.* First, the star's position is measured against what we believe to be distant background objects. Then another measurement of the star's apparent position is made six months later, when the Earth has traveled to the other side of its orbit around the Sun. This gives astronomers a baseline of 186 million miles (299 million kilometers) between the two points of the Earth's orbit. They actually take many measurements until they determine which ones represent the longest baselines for a particular object. Even with such baselines, inaccuracies can occur because of the Earth's atmosphere and limitations of the equipment. These numbers in astronomy are rounded off.

The accuracy of trigonometric parallax for distances of up to 10 light-years from the Earth is within 3 percent. There are only eleven stars known within this range, and three of them are in the same system: Alpha Centauri. At a distance of 30 light-years, the accuracy of measurements is believed to be plus or minus 10 percent. Distances of stars that are 100 light-years away can be off by 30 percent, and this distance is generally considered the limit for reasonably accurate measurements.

Measuring the Galaxy

If 100 light-years is the usual limit for such trigonometric techniques, then how do astronomers measure our Milky Way, which has a diameter estimated at 100,000 light-years? By collecting the light of distant stars on photographic plates and studying their spectra—a technique called *stellar spectroscopy.* Nearby stars whose distances have been measured with parallax can be used to match similar stars which are at greater distances. These appear to be dim, but they are only farther away. Once a distant star's spectral type has been determined and compared with closer stars, its actual brightness can be determined. Once its actual brightness and its brightness from Earth are known, distance can be estimated. This indirect method of determining distance is called *spectroscopic parallax.*

Many thousands of stars have been given distance estimates throughout our Milky Way Galaxy by studying the spectra of their light.

A Better Yardstick

The European Space Agency plans to launch a special satellite in 1988 that will greatly improve the accuracy of cosmic measurements. Named Hipparcos, the satellite has one goal: to accurately measure the angular positions of stars in the sky. It will measure some 100,000 stars with an accuracy ten times that of today's Earth-based telescopes. This means that the sample of stars whose distance can be reliably measured will be increased by a factor of a thousand and will include many unique star types for the first time. The wealth of data will all be automatically processed on Earth, so that thousands of stars can be measured at one time. Future starship crews will know how long the trip will take.

A Disfigured Sky

If all the stars in the sky—the three to four thousand seen by the human eye under ideal conditions—were to have apparent motions equal to Barnard's star, one of the fastest in the sky, then all the familiar constellations would become disfigured and unrecognizable in a few hundred years. In the beginning of such stellar motions, hunter Orion's belt would sag, Queen Cassiopeia's throne would crumble, Sagittarius' bow would snap, and virgin Virgo's wings would wilt. Ultimately all the celestial myths and images would be lost to even the most imaginative stargazers.

The Pleiades Unraveled

The famous Pleiades open star cluster, made up of the conspicuous six or seven naked-eye stars and more than three hundred telescopic ones, was one of the first groups of stars to be mentioned in world literature. The Chinese annals of 2357 B.C. refer to it, as do the Bible (in the Book of Job) and Homer's *Odyssey.*

All the stars in the Pleiades cluster are physically associated and move through space together in the same direction. Since the Pleiades cluster is probably the most photographed astronomical object of all time, with photographs dating back more than one hundred years, astronomers had a time-lapse photo sequence, from which they determined the concerted movement of the cluster. Long-exposure photographs also showed what the naked eye or telescope often could not detect: a wispy nebulosity left over from the gaseous cloud that formed the stars. This nebulosity, and the fact that most of the stars are hot and white main-sequence stars, gives the Pleiades an age of approximately 50 million years, which means they began shining approximately when the Earth was greening with its first grass.

Open star clusters, however, are known to be short-lived as cosmic lifetimes go, and their stars eventually break away from one another and go their separate ways. The Pleiades

This wisp of hydrogen gas in the famous Pleiades cluster was left over when these young stars were born—about the same time the first grass grew on Earth. *Courtesy Mount Wilson and Las Campanas Observatories of the Carnegie Institution of Washington.*

cluster is no exception; it will lose its identity as a cluster in perhaps 1 billion years, and no longer will the Pleiades (as Tennyson said in "Locksley Hall")

> Glitter like a swarm of fireflies
> tangled in a silver braid.

Even the silver braid will unravel in time.

Celestial Couples

The nearest twenty-six visible stars, including the Sun, become thirty-six stars when optical instruments are aimed at them, and there are probably other small and dim ones that remain undetected. With a pair of binoculars or a small telescope, many visual pairs are observed easily. Astronomers believe that at least half the "stars" in the sky are multiple-star systems, including doubles, triples, and even more complicated groupings.

One of the most interesting local systems is the naked-eye star Zeta Ursae Majoris (in the constellation of the Great Bear, commonly known as the Big Dipper). Zeta, the central star in the Dipper's handle, is actually two stars: Mizar and Alcor. Bright, second-magnitude Mizar is accompanied by tiny, fourth-magnitude Alcor. Also called the "Horse and Rider," this pair was known to fourteenth-century Arabian writers as Al Sadak ("the Test" or "the Riddle"). It was used to test eyesight. Even though the human eye may be challenged to separate their images, their cosmic distance from one another is about a quarter of a light-year—enough space to line up some eight thousand solar systems between them.

Go outside on a cold, crisp evening and look for the Horse and Rider. They will only be a blink of an eye apart.

Near Neighbors

In the southern sky, in the constellation Centaurus, one of the finest visual double stars in the sky can be seen: Alpha and Beta Centauri. Both are bright, first-magnitude stars. A faint companion star of Alpha, Proxima Centauri, makes this a triple-star system. Proxima has the greatest proper motion against the stellar background of any star in the sky found to date. This puts Proxima about 4.34 light-years away from the Sun—about 25 trillion miles (40 trillion kilometers)—and makes it the closest star to the Sun yet discovered.

Little Proxima, a red dwarf, is one of the dimmest stars known, probably thirteen thousand times dimmer than the Sun. It is thought that about ten thousand astronomical units (the average Sun-Earth distance) separate Alpha and Proxima Centauri. If there are any Proxima Centaurians and they look toward the constellation Camelopardalis, the Giraffe, they will see a bright star about one and a half times as bright as Alpha appears to us. It is our Sun. Because of the closeness of this triple system to our place in the Milky Way, with a few minor changes for the very brightest stars in their sky, Proxima Centaurians would be comfortable using our naked-eye star charts.

The daytime sky for Proxima Centaurians, though, would be quite different. From a planet circling Proxima, their star would only be a dim sun emitting light equal to about twenty-four of our full Moons. But even more unusual to us would be the other two suns in the sky, Alpha and Beta, one brighter and one dimmer than our Sun. Because of these three stars in their skies, their time system would probably be much more complicated than our own.

How Bright the Light?

When astronomers speak of the apparent magnitude of a star or other celestial object, they are referring to an ancient system of comparing star brightnesses first used by Hipparchus and then Ptolemy, some two thousand years ago. It refers to what we actually see in the sky. Although the basic concept of this magnitude system remains largely unchanged today, it is now based on precise measurements of stars whose brightnesses are known.

Apparent magnitude is based upon a scale of ratios of brightness, and each magnitude represents a change in apparent brightness of about 2.5 times. Brighter objects have lower numbers. For example, our Sun, the brightest object in the sky, has a magnitude of -26.7; the full Moon's magnitude is -12; Sirius, the brightest star in the sky, is -1.5, and the dimmest stars that most of us can see are about magnitude $+6$, although some people with excellent eyesight and ideal dark skies can see to magnitude $+7$.

A difference of five magnitudes between two stars

means that the lower-magnitude star is one hundred times brighter than the other star. Our Sun, at magnitude -26.7, is 3 trillion times brighter than a magnitude $+7$ star.

As if all this were not confusing enough, astronomers also refer to an object's absolute magnitude, which is the apparent magnitude of a star or other cosmic object if it were at a distance of 32.6 light-years (10 parsecs). The difference between a star's apparent magnitude and its absolute magnitude is important in measuring cosmic distances.

The Nearest Star
Is Very Far

When we use light-years as if they were miles or kilometers, we lose our cosmic perspective. If you wanted to take a trip in a car to Proxima Centauri, the nearest star, some 4.34 light-years away, how long would it take? Way too long!

Traveling at 55 miles (88 kilometers) an hour, this magical car could cover 482,000 miles (775,500 kilometers) each year. At this rate, the journey would take some 52 million years. If this cosmic trip began at the time *Homo sapiens* began appearing on the planet, then less than one eightieth of the journey would be completed by now, and more than 24,000 generations would have lived out their lives along the way.

Galactic Demographics

Most astronomers agree that the average mass of a star in the Galaxy is about 50 percent of our Sun's mass. There is also general agreement that the Galaxy has a mass equal to at least 100 billion Suns. If these numbers are correct, then there are over 200 billion stars in the galactic halo, core, and disk. The halo would have 40 billion stars, the core 80 billion, and the disk another 80 billion. The disk, however, is the only area of the Galaxy that shows growth potential, and the stellar birthrate and population of this area are expected to remain high.

The Stellar Majority

There are giant stars, dwarf stars; hot stars, cool stars; white, red, and brown stars; pulsing stars, exploding stars; gestating stars, dying stars; and more—more colors, sizes, and endless variations on these themes. The majority of these stars, approximately 90 percent of them, are known as *main-sequence stars*—a grouping in which they spend the greater part of their lifetimes. That means that nine out of ten individual stars selected from the thousands visible in the sky or the countless millions on long-exposure photographic plates would fit into this sequence group, and a star's position in this sequence tells a great deal about its age, size (volume and mass), brightness, color, and temperature. The main sequence was discovered and depicted graphically by two astronomers working separately in the early 1900s, Hertzsprung and Russell, who plotted the relationship between brightness and spectral types of nearby stars on a graph (see next section, "Sorting Out the Stars").

Our Sun—yellow, not too hot, middle-sized, and in midlife—falls just about in the middle of the main sequence. Protostars—those in the process of forming but not yet hot enough to begin nuclear fusion—have not yet reached the main sequence. The red giants, supergiants, and white dwarfs, at the other extreme, have left the main sequence and are dying. But in between is most of a star's life, and it is a star's mass (not volume, but mass) that determines where it falls on this sequence. The hottest and brightest stars begin the sequence, and the coolest red dwarfs end it. Colors range from blue-white hot (O stars, up to 40,000 degrees Celsius, 72,000 degrees Fahrenheit) to orange-red cool (M stars, 3,000 degrees Celsius, 5,400 degrees Fahrenheit). Main-sequence star sizes range from one tenth the diameter of the Sun (about the size of Jupiter) to ten times the Sun's diameter (almost 9 million miles, 14.5 million kilometers, or forty times the Earth-Moon distance). Main-sequence star densities range from about one tenth to about three times the density of water. Off the main sequence are the collapsed stars— white dwarfs, neutron stars, and black holes—and the rare stellar freaks—giants, supergiants, and protostars.

When astronomy students say, "Oh! Be a fine girl, kiss me," they are not making an egghead's pass but, rather, learning the spectral classes of the main-sequence stars: O-B-A-F-G-K-M. This Harvard system of spectral classification is based on the Draper Catalogue, which lists the spectra of more than 225,000 stars. By reading starlight—a star's spectrum—astronomers can tell almost everything they've always wanted to know about an individual star in the stellar majority.

Sorting Out the Stars

The major differences between O, B, A, F, G, K, and M stars are differences in temperature and mass, which are related—from the big, hot O stars to the small, cool M stars. The important relationship between a star's temperature and color (derived from its spectrum) and its brightness (absolute magnitude as compared to the Sun) was independently established soon after the turn of the century by Ejnar Hertzsprung, a Danish astronomer, and Henry Russell, an American astronomer. They first plotted the spectral class (color and temperature) and the luminosity of stars on a graph, luminosity on the vertical axis and temperature on the horizontal axis.

That the vast majority of plotted stars appeared in a well-defined path that ran diagonally across the graph from upper left to lower right was an important finding: it defined a large family of stars called the main sequence. In some diagrams (not pictured here), above the main sequence, across the top of the diagram, are the extreme supergiants, which may be

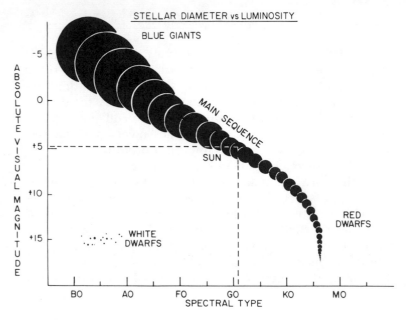

STELLAR DIAMETER vs LUMINOSITY

Various relationships between certain types of stars—their brightness, temperature, and spectral class—are plotted on Hertzsprung-Russell diagrams, one of astronomy's most important tools. *Courtesy Science Graphics,* © *1985.*

fifty thousand times brighter than the Sun. Below these, in what would be the upper-right corner of our diagram, are the aging red giants, while the lower-left corner represents the white dwarfs—degenerate, dying stars.

In honor of Hertzsprung and Russell, this type of diagram—one of the most important tools in astronomy of which there are many versions for many different kinds of problems—was called the Hertzsprung-Russell diagram (often abbreviated to H-R diagram).

The extremes of brightness, temperature, and mass between stars on the main sequence can be seen in two stars at opposite ends of the H-R diagram. At the upper left, O-type Delta Orionis, which is the westernmost star of the three in

Orion's belt, blazes twenty thousand times brighter than the Sun, has a 28,000-degree Celsius (50,000-degree Fahrenheit) temperature, and has a diameter thirty times larger than the Sun. Barnard's star, on the lower-right corner of the H-R main sequence, is an M-type red dwarf that shines feebly at one twenty-five-hundredth the intensity of the Sun, has a

Barnard's star, a dim red star, will outlive most other stars in the sky, including our Sun. It also has one of the largest proper motions in the sky, which is shown here over a period of ten years. A Lick Observatory Photograph. *Courtesy Lick Observatory.*

surface temperature of about 3,000 degrees Celsius (5,400 degrees Fahrenheit), and has a mass only one sixth the Sun's. In the stellar world, lifetimes vary greatly. The life spans of these two main-sequence stars are representative of all stars: the heavier, brighter stars burn out much faster than the smaller, dimmer stars. Dim Barnard's star will outlive Delta Orionis by as many as 5 trillion years.

Stellar Nurseries

Stars are born in the dense, dark clouds of gas and dust scattered throughout the Milky Way and other galaxies, especially in the spiral arms. When these clouds are described as "dense," the word is used relatively to more empty cosmic space. Their density is estimated to be only about one hydrogen atom per cubic centimeter, or about 360,000 hydrogen atoms in a volume of interstellar space equal to the volume of a garbage can. Compared to the best vacuum producible on Earth, this is absolutely empty space; yet in space it is rich enough to spawn stars.

A number of processes are believed to be at work in the star nurseries. Giant molecular clouds of mostly hydrogen gas and tiny cosmic dust grains (such as the beautiful Great Nebula of Orion, M42, visible through small telescopes) have ideal conditions for producing newborn stars.

Many young stars are found in these clouds, cuddled by a blanket of dark, obscuring dust and gas. About twenty have recently been found in the cloud known as the Ophiuchus Complex, situated in the constellation of Ophiuchus, the Serpent-Bearer. These young stars appear to be visually dimmed by a hundred magnitudes. This means that their light has been dimmed almost 400 billion times by the surrounding gas and dust.

A Cool, Slow Birth

Interstellar clouds contract, very slowly, because of the gravitational force. Each grain of dust or molecule of gas is attracted toward the center of the cloud, as if all the other grains were there. Slowly, very slowly, the cold, dark matter condenses into what is known as a *protostar.*

Depending on the mass of the cloud, the protostar can be formed in as little time as 100,000 years or take 1 million

Giant molecular clouds of mostly hydrogen and dust are the birthplace of many new stars. This is a section of the Rosette Nebula (NGC 2237), in the constellation Monoceros. A Palomar Observatory Photograph. *Courtesy California Institute of Technology.*

years or longer. The larger clouds, because of their extra mass, will form more quickly, due to stronger gravitational forces. There is, however, a limit to how long this protostar phase can last. Again, depending on mass and gravity, the protostar will either develop into a real star in about 15 million years, or not make the grade if it is too small. Experts believe that if the object is less than one sixth the Sun's size (less than the mass of twenty thousand Earths), or sixty times larger than the mass of our giant planet Jupiter, it cannot become a star. The nuclear fires will never ignite, and the almost-star will flicker and die. It is estimated that our Sun would have burned for only 10 million to 100 million years if just the heat of gravitational contraction fueled it. Because this time period is much less than the known geological history of planet Earth, we know that a process involving nuclear reactions is taking place.

As the temperature rises in the condensing protostar, it begins to glow like a furnace. This can occur at temperatures of several million degrees. The heat creates an outward pressure which encounters the inward press of gravity. Gradually the density and temperature rise and more matter is attracted.

These infant stars are still wreathed in their obscuring dust and, though glowing softly, are often invisible to astronomers at optical wavelengths of light. By using telescopes and orbiting statellites which detect light in the infrared region, the protostars can be discovered hiding within their dusty cocoons.

The Molecular Hideout

Molecular astronomy, a young branch of the science that came into its own in the 1970s, searches for molecular groupings in the cold interstellar gas and dust clouds of the Galaxy. Most of the molecules are discovered by radio astronomers in dark, dense clouds, where they are shielded from the destructive ultraviolet rays of neighboring stars. There, interstellar atoms couple with other atoms to form molecules on the surface of cold (−173 degrees Celsius, −279 degrees Fahrenheit) interstellar particles. In these thick, dark clouds, more than 16 billion particles could fit into every cubic inch (1 billion per cubic centimeter), but it takes as long as 100,000 years for a molecule to condense out of the gas and adhere to one of these microscopic specks of dust.

From Clouds to Globs

The late astronomer Bart J. Bok, a world authority on the Milky Way Galaxy, believed that the condensing clouds contracted into dark blobs of dust in which stars were born. These Bok globules can sometimes be seen through larger optical telescopes as they stand out against the brighter Milky Way background. It is estimated that they have a mass of twenty to two hundred Suns and a volume ranging from as

The condensing clouds contract into dark blobs of dust and gas known as Bok globules, named after the famous authority on the Milky Way Galaxy, Bart Bok. This dark cloudlet may become a new star within a million years. *Courtesy Yerkes Observatory.*

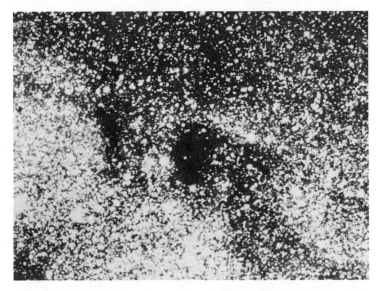

large as a cubic parsec (3.26^3 light-years) to as small as a volume equaling ninety Solar Systems. The dark globule may change from a small, dark cloudlet to a newborn star in as little as 1 million years. That is only 570,000 times the gestation period of an elephant and 1.3 million times that of a human baby.

Stellar Impregnation

Sometimes the large molecular clouds are near bright clusters of stars. Their ultraviolet radiation creates pressure eddies as it passes through the cloud. This may be enough, over tens of thousands of years, to begin the cloud's collapse that forms protostars. An example of this process can be seen in the bright, reddish Lagoon Nebula (M8), in the constellation Sagittarius, the Archer.

It is as if the older star cluster is actually seeding the cloud with its energy and beginning the gestation period for a new generation of stars.

A Cosmic Firecracker

One of the most spectacular events ever seen by humankind was recorded by Chinese astronomers more than nine hundred years ago. A supernova explosion, caused by a dying star, seen in A.D. 1054 left behind its remnants and formed the famous Crab Nebula (M1, or NGC 1952). The Crab is an expanding cloud resembling a Fourth of July starburst, and it has a surprise at its center: a rotating neutron star, also known as a pulsar.

Such events can cause stars to form when the interstellar gas and dust between the stars is stirred and begins to condense into protostars. The process could happen quickly, in about 100,000 years, but this would be rare. More often, it would take ten to one hundred times that long.

Cosmic collisions between two gas and dust clouds can also form stars. These clouds ebb and flow within our galaxy at speeds of about 2,500 miles (4,022 kilometers) an hour.

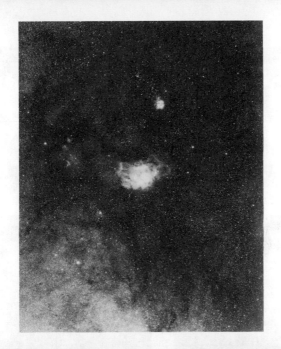

Two views of the bright reddish Lagoon Nebula (M8), in the constellation Sagittarius. The ultraviolet radiation from the bright clusters of stars creates pressure eddies that begin the cloud's collapse. A Palomar Observatory Photograph, and a Lick Observatory Photograph. *Courtesy California Institute of Technology and courtesy Lick Observatory.*

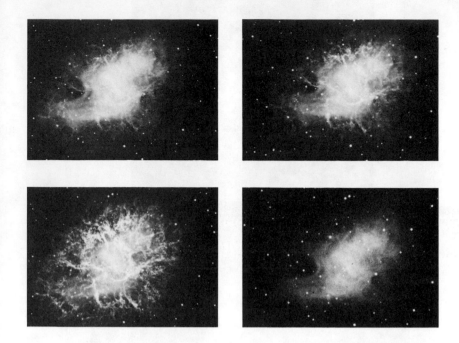

Chinese astronomers recorded the Crab supernova more than nine hundred years ago, in A.D. 1054. These four photographs are taken in infrared, red, yellow, and blue light. *Courtesy Mount Wilson and Las Campanas Observatories of the Carnegie Institution of Washington.*

A Stellar Babe Is Born

A star baby arrived in the Milky Way during 1936 and 1937. In the winter constellation Orion, the Hunter, near the bright, first-magnitude giant star Betelgeuse (the Hunter's left shoulder), the star FU Orionis was first observed. Astronomers believe it is a brand-new star, sending its message of light to Earth. The small star's cocoon of dark dust was seen to glow when the star brightened in 1937—a birth announcement across the light-years.

A number of other suspected newborns have been discovered since then, and they are usually associated with small, bright nebulae.

Another rich stellar nursery filled with the life-blood of the Universe—hydrogen—which when compressed allows thermonuclear fusion to take place and stars to burn. *Courtesy The Anglo-Australian Observatory,* © *1979.*

How Born Yonder Star?

While many astronomers believe that all stars form from dark clouds of interstellar matter, others believe that hot blobs of electrically charged gas (ionized gas), created by the condensations of the original materials of the Universe, formed the first stars, and that the following star generations came from the dark clouds.

Still other astronomers think that violent explosions in the centers of galaxies create the bright spiral arms and their young, hot stars. It is probable that stars are born in various ways during different ages and different conditions of the Universe.

Main Street, Universe

About 90 percent of the stars we can see are what astronomers call main-sequence stars. When stars are plotted on a Hertzsprung-Russell diagram by color and temperature, the main-sequence stars fall into a diagonal grouping, from the upper left to the lower right on the diagram. It represents the Main Street of the Universe, where most stars spend most of their lives. A main-sequence star, astronomers now know, burns hydrogen in its core. Its position on the main sequence tells astronomers that it is a young or middle-aged star and that it has a long life, measured in millions or billions of years, before it dies. Our Sun is only one star in billions that live on this stellar Main Street.

When stars like the Sun leave the hydrogen-helium cycle, their color (temperature) and brightness change and they leave the main sequence. How long a particular star remains on the main sequence, burning hydrogen fuel, depends on its mass. Larger stars burn faster and hotter, and they may live on Main Street for only 1 million years. Small, cool stars may stay on their hydrogen diet for 10 billion years —about the age of the Milky Way Galaxy. Some of these small, ancient stars still exist, strewn behind in the vast corona of our galaxy. Almost invisible to most astronomical instruments, these stars add a great deal of mass to the Galaxy, even though they do not call attention to themselves as do the giants, supergiants, exploding novae, and supernovae that transmit great messages of light toward planet Earth.

The Old Red Giants

Once the hydrogen in the cores of dwarf stars like our Sun is completely consumed, the cores begin to collapse, and their outer envelopes, still containing hydrogen fuel and still sustaining fusion, expand in volume to three or four hundred times the size of the Sun. The dense dwarf has become a rarefied red giant.

The great red Betelgeuse, a first-magnitude star also known as Alpha Orionis, is the most famous red giant. Its volume is more than 160 million times that of the Sun. This beautiful star is so large and tenuous that its average density is less than one 100-millionth that of the Sun and one ten-thousandth the density of the Earth's atmosphere.

Those Middle-Class Degenerates: White Dwarfs

Stars about the size of our Sun that have burned up all their hydrogen and have undergone gravitational collapse are called white dwarfs. After collapse, the atoms of white dwarf stars are jammed so tightly together that a thimbleful of their star stuff would weigh more than 10 tons. This inconceivable compression also strips the electrons from the nuclei of the atoms and creates what is known as degenerate matter.

These are dying stars, and they glow because of the intense heat generated by their enormous pressures after gravitational collapse. Actually they may not be white in color at all, but can range from yellow to red. As they slowly die over millions of years, they eventually become brown or black dwarfs—dark cinders of suns lost in the Galaxy's light.

Heavy Dwarfs

One of the most interesting white dwarfs is Van Maanen's star, which can be seen through small telescopes. Located about 13.8 light-years away and about 2 degrees south of the star Delta Piscium, in the constellation Pisces, it is almost six thousand times dimmer than our Sun. Its surface temperature, however, is about the same as our Sun's: 6,000 degrees Celsius (10,800 degrees Fahrenheit).

Van Maanen's star is one of the smallest stars known; it is about the size of our planet Earth. Its mass, however, is estimated to be equal to that of the Sun. This means that a cubic inch (16 cubic centimeters) of its star stuff would weigh some 20 tons—about the weight of a cement truck holding 3 cubic yards of cement. A trowelful of this white dwarf's matter would weigh about 100 tons.

White dwarfs are among the oldest stars known, and Van Maanen's star is one of the oldest known objects in the Universe. Its nuclear fires may have burned out 4 to 5 billion years ago, about the time our Sun began to shine and long before the Earth existed.

Flashy Dwarfs

Some stars suddenly increase their brightness by as much as ten thousand times, and for a short time equal some of the most brilliant giant stars in the Galaxy. They are known as novae, from the Latin *stella nova* (new star).

Novae are believed to be white dwarfs in close orbit or even physical contact with red giant stars. As the cooler, large giant loses matter to its smaller, denser companion, the hydrogen-rich gas forms a disk around the little star. Eventu-

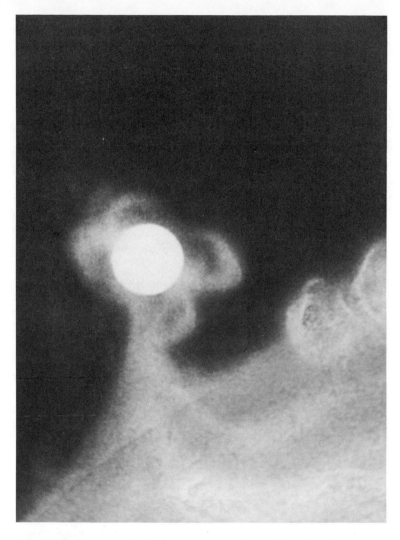

Nova explosions are believed to occur when white dwarf stars are close to giant stars and pull hydrogen away from the rarefied giants. When the energy-rich hydrogen builds up to a point . . . BOOM! From the film *The Universe, courtesy NASA*.

ally enough of the energy-rich hydrogen collects to cause the nova flare—perhaps because of runaway hydrogen fusion in the dwarf's upper layers.

From ten to thirty novae are believed to occur in the Milky Way each year, and several are usually visible each year in small telescopes. Every ten years or so, one is visible to the unaided eye. A recent nova was Nova Cygni (in the constellation Cygnus, the Swan), which occurred in 1975. A

Nova Cygni occurred in 1975. From ten to thirty novae are believed to occur in our galaxy each year. Note the tremendous decline of brightness over just a few days. A Lick Observatory Photograph. *Courtesy Lick Observatory.*

The expanding debris from Nova Persei, which occurred in 1901. This photo was taken in 1949, so the stuff had had forty-eight years to fly outward. A Palomar Observatory Photograph. *Courtesy California Institute of Technology.*

nova flash occurs suddenly, at least relative to cosmic sizes, often in less than a day. Then its brilliance gradually fades over months or sometimes years to its original luminosity. Some stars host novae more than once, but they do not receive new life in the process just because they have the episodes of brilliance; they are still essentially dying stars.

Galactic Blasts: Supernovae

About every hundred years in our galaxy, two or three giant stars that are ten times the size of our Sun collapse and explode. These cosmic events, called supernovae, blast away most of the stars' matter and flash a stupendous radiance across the light-years. This gravitational collapse is over in less than a minute, and what remains is a neutron star, its matter compressed to a small sphere of 6 to 20 miles (10 to 30 kilometers) in diameter. Again, it is the mass of the original star that determines the way a star will die, and the neutron star is midway between a white-dwarf death and the black-hole demise for larger stars.

In the winter constellation of Taurus, the Bull, there is the most easily seen supernova remnant, the Crab Nebula (M1, NGC 1952). Because this object also emits X rays, it is known as Taurus X-1 as well. In a small telescope, the Crab can be seen as a strange, dim oval. In long-exposure photographs, it resembles a Fourth of July fireworks explosion that has been frozen in time.

Chinese astronomers recorded the Crab supernova in the year A.D. 1054, but it was not until the twentieth century that astronomers discovered a neutron star spinning rapidly at its center. The Crab's gas and dust expands at a rate of more than 50 million miles (80 million kilometers) a day. Much of this exploding star stuff is composed of elements heavier than the original elements of hydrogen and helium. These heavier elements, which were forged in the core of the star during its lifetime, are what create a rich, fertile ground for future star birth.

Our Milky Way is long overdue for a supernova. The eccentric Danish astronomer Tycho Brahe discovered one in 1572, and his assistant, Johannes Kepler, recorded one in 1604. The next supernova in our galaxy will probably be discovered by the human eye without the help of a telescope, because the odds are high for a bright one.

The exact date that the Crab's supernova radiance reached the Earth? July 4, A.D. 1054.

Deadly Danger

If a supernova flared within two to three light-years of the Earth, it would kill all life with its deadly bath of high-

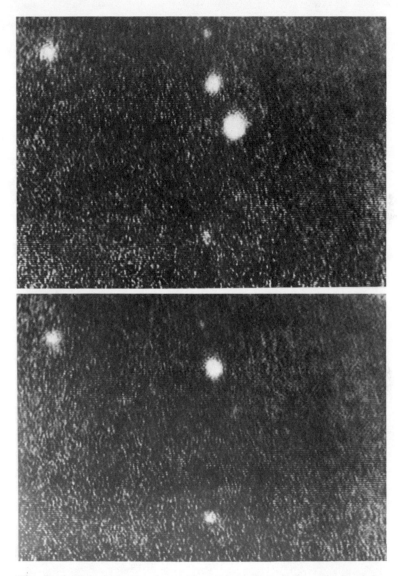

The Crab Nebula pulsar (neutron star) was left at the center of the explosion in A.D. 1054. It is seen here at its maximum and minimum pulses. One pulsar/neutron star rotates more than six hundred times every second. *Courtesy Lick Observatory.*

energy radiation. This is why the great gulfs of space between the stars are a blessing for life on Earth, but much less of one if humankind cannot control its own deadly radiations.

Pulsar Population Explosion

Pulsars are what radio astronomers hear when they tune in to neutron stars, the remaining collapsed star core after a supernova explosion. A recent study suggests that there may be as many as two hundred thousand pulsars in the Milky Way Galaxy.

For a pulsar (neutron star) to exist, the star core must be larger than 1.4 solar masses after the supernova explosion. If it is smaller, it will die the white-dwarf death. Astrophysical theory states that such a star core would be so compressed that its atoms would be in the form of a crystalline solid that resembles diamond.

The pulsars are spinning very rapidly because of a scientific principle called conservation of angular momentum, the same thing that causes ice skaters to spin more rapidly when they draw in their arms. The spinning star has an enormous magnetic field and sprays matter like a hose or a lighthouse as it turns. If we are in the right position, our instruments will see the rapid pulses.

How fast do pulsars rotate? Some have rotational rates of about fourteen seconds; others rotate more than a hundred times a second. It is estimated that a new pulsar (neutron star) appears in the Galaxy once every 30 to 120 years. This is the same frequency range as supernovae and for the demise of giant stars that leave the neutron stars behind.

Tick Tock, Tick Tock

Pulsars spin with such regularity that—even though they slow down slightly over time—they can be used as clocks. The fastest of all pulsars, PSR 1937 + 21, is rotating 642 times per second (once every 1.56 thousandths of a second). Discovered in 1982, this object is almost as reliable as the best atomic clock. The star is spinning some 55 million times faster than the main gear in a grandfather's clock.

A Clock Gone Wild

One of the principal characteristics of the rapidly spinning, X-ray-emitting pulsars is that their pulsations are very regular and predictable—as accurate as an atomic clock. Or so astronomers thought until recently.

A group of European astronomers have found "quasiperiodic emissions" in an X-ray source called GX5-1. They observed a series of pulses with differing periods. This may make GX5-1 the first of a class of new objects that astronomers have called quasiperiodic objects (QPOs). First observed by the X-ray-detecting satellite *Exosat,* GX5-1 was found to have groups of pulses ranging from twenty to forty oscillations per second. After this discovery, other quasiperiodic pulsations were found in other well-known X-ray sources in the Galaxy, Scorpio X-1 and Cygnus X-2. Some astronomers believe that these variations are not caused by the star's changing its rotation period but, rather, by material from an orbiting accretion disk falling into the star and creating the apparently variable "beat." The rotation period of GX5-1 is about 10.5 milliseconds, which means it is spinning about a hundred times a second.

Brown Dwarfs:
The Almost Stars

Brown dwarf objects have been predicted by astrophysical theory but never actually observed. This could change, however, when the Hubble Space Telescope and other sophisticated astronomical instruments begin observing above the Earth's atmosphere.

Brown dwarfs are believed to be protostars that do not

have enough mass to ever ignite their nuclear fires. The Universe could be full of them, but they would be so dim, emitting only faint infrared radiation caused by their dissipating heat, that astronomers cannot find them.

Some experts make the case that we have a brown dwarf right here in our solar system: Jupiter. The giant planet produces twice as much heat as it receives from the Sun, and it may have even glowed for a time before flickering out. Jupiter, much larger than all the other planets combined, is the largest object in the Solar System next to the Sun. Its composition is also very much like a star's: about 90 percent hydrogen and 10 percent helium. If Jupiter were only sixty times more massive, it would have moved past the protostar phase and become a second star in our solar system. Instead, giant Jupiter has a constant, cold surface temperature of about -138 degrees Celsius (-216 degrees Fahrenheit).

Brown dwarfs are far removed from black holes in the cosmic cast of characters. While brown dwarfs are almost-stars that never ignited, black holes are massive stars, at least 3.2 times the size of our Sun, that have had a complete gravitational collapse—a kind of cosmic coronary.

The Phantom Black Holes

The popular Walt Disney movie aside, do black holes really exist? A good many astronomers give a 90 percent probability that at least one has been found: Cygnus X-1, an intense X-ray source in the constellation of the same name, and other candidates continue to be discovered and scrutinized. Still, some astronomers sit on the black-hole fence and await the wealth of new research data that will be flowing from the Hubble Space Telescope and other above-the-Earth satellites and observatories. No self-respecting observational astronomer took black holes seriously before the mid-1960s, but that attitude changed when pulsars were discovered late in the decade and were shown to be rotating neutron stars—up to that time another theoretical stellar type.

Since black holes are literally out of sight, forming after a large star ends its fusion life and collapses, taking all light and other radiation with it, never again to escape, how can astronomers detect them? Mainly with patience. First, by homing in on a distant X-ray source with in-orbit instruments. Second, by matching it to an optical star that is known by its motions to have an invisible partner. Third, by proceeding slowly, carefully, painstakingly with the cosmic detective work, which can take thousands of astronomer-hours and many years to reach a qualified, good-bet answer.

When a large star, more than three times the mass of our Sun, collapses at the end of its life, a black hole is created, from which nothing (not even light) can escape. From the film *The Universe*, *courtesy NASA.*

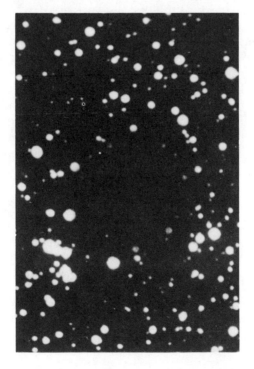

A Black Hole for the 1980s

The Copernicus satellite, an ultraviolet and X-ray observatory launched in the early 1970s, discovered a potential black hole in 1978 in the constellation Scorpius: V861 Scorpii. Unlike Cygnus X-1, its X-ray source disappears *completely* once every orbit, eclipsed by either the supergiant star companion or the gas stream that flows from it to the accretion disk around the probable black hole. This implies that the two-body stellar system is almost edge-on to Earth and allows a more accurate determination of the invisible object's mass than does the Cygnus X-1 binary system, whose exact orbital perspective from Earth is in doubt. While much more research is needed before astronomers know V861 Scorpii as well as Cygnus X-1, they have calculated its mass as between seven and eleven times that of the Sun, well above the collapsed-neutron-star limit of 3.2 solar masses, which puts it in the class of ultimate stellar degenerates—black holes—where gravity takes absolute and final dominance over matter and from which nothing can ever escape: no radiation, no matter, nothing.

If the hypothetical starship *Robert Goddard* and its crew passed across this black hole's gravitational boundary (event horizon), there would be no escape. The ship and the people aboard would be infinitely crushed and broken down into subatomic particles. As density climbed beyond 10 billion tons per cubic inch, even the neutrons would break down into smaller subatomic particles called hyperons. No one, ever, in any amount of time, could put the *Robert Goddard* and its crew back together again.

Avoiding Horizons

If the Sun were a black hole, it would not wrench the planets from their orbits and devour them, as might be expected. Although the Earth and the other planets would become dark and cold, they would continue to orbit the black hole, safely away from any dangerous gravitational pull, which begins at the black hole's boundary, the so-called event horizon. Nothing can escape from inside the event horizon to the outside. This hypothetical black hole would have an event horizon of only 3.6 miles (5.8 kilometers) diameter, but it would still retain the gravitational power of our blazing, life-giving star. Just as today's aircraft pilot must respect the horizon, so must future spacefarers respect the event horizons of collapsed stars.

Evaporating Black Holes

The British physicist Stephen Hawking has shown in recent theoretical work that black holes evaporate over great time periods. A black hole like the one in Cygnus X-1 (estimated at about ten solar masses) would take 10^{66} years to evaporate—the number 1 followed by 66 zeros—which is to say millions of times longer than the estimated age of the Universe, about 18 billion years. If the Universe oscillates, first expanding, then contracting, no large black hole will ever have time to evaporate—including the gigantic one scientists suspect is at the center of the Galaxy.

CHAPTER 2

THE GALACTIC NEIGHBORHOOD

Prais'd be the fathomless universe,
For life and joy, and for objects and knowledge
curious. . . .

> —Walt Whitman,
> *When Lilacs Last in the Dooryard Bloom'd*

Our Galaxy's Neighbors

Most of the 100 billion or more galaxies in the Universe have local neighbors and are members of either a small group or a larger cluster. Our home galaxy, the Milky Way, belongs to a small group of galaxies called the Local Group, which is composed of perhaps as many as thirty galaxies: large spirals, dwarf ellipticals, and irregulars.

The overall shape of our Local Group of galaxies is not spherical, like some of the more distant and larger clusters, but irregular. Most of the galaxy members are concentrated around two of the group's largest members—the Milky Way and the Andromeda Galaxy—with the recently discovered Maffei 1 elliptical now marking a far boundary. These two great spirals dominate the present view of the Local Group and account for upward of 70 percent of the total mass.

Our Local Group of galaxies is a sparse community, and its members have plenty of space in which to move, unlike the distant rich clusters of galaxies, where densities are high and gravitational wars—and some actual physical contact—are not uncommon. While our Local Group has been labeled "poor" in total number of galaxies, it contains the only galaxy known to harbor life, which makes it unique in the cosmic realm of galaxy clusters. Our learning about this vast neighborhood is in itself astounding.

Astronomers have given various values for the Local Group's diameter in the past, usually 2 to 3 million light-years, primarily based on the distance between the two great spirals—the Milky Way and Andromeda (M31)—that appear to be subclusters in the Local Group. But if the Maffei 1 Galaxy, discovered in 1968, is taken into account and its distance measured from the dwarf elliptical NGC 6822, the farthest local member from it, the Local Group's diameter is almost 5 million light-years. If a light-year is represented by 1 inch (2.54 centimeters), then the diameter of the Milky Way Galaxy would be about 1.6 miles (2.54 kilometers), and the diameter of our local galactic neighborhood would be 79 miles (127 kilometers).

If a light-year is represented by an inch (2.54 centimeters), then the neighborhood of our Local Group of galaxies would be about 79 miles (127 kilometers) in diameter. *Courtesy Science Graphics,* © *1985.*

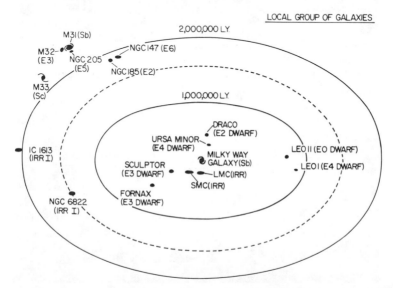

The Local Trillion-Plus

The total mass of the galaxies in the Local Group is estimated to equal at least 700 billion Suns. If the average star is about half the mass of our Sun, this means that there may be as many as 1.5 trillion stars in our Local Group alone.

Naked-Eye Galaxies

Five galaxies in the Local Group can be seen without the help of binoculars or telescopes. This is not a well-known fact, especially among city and suburban dwellers that have light-polluted skies. Our own Milky Way, of course, is the galaxy seen by almost everyone who has been under dark skies when the Moon is down. The next-brightest galaxies are the Clouds of Magellan, the Large and Small Magellanic Clouds,

The two Magellanic Clouds, satellite galaxies to our Milky Way spiral, are separated by 80,000 light-years. From the southern hemisphere, they can be seen with the naked eye. *Courtesy Yerkes Observatory.*

which are visible from the Earth's southern hemisphere, being above our planet's south pole. These beautiful sky glows were first recorded by Portuguese sailors in 1519 and named after the great Portuguese explorer Ferdinand Magellan. They are bright celestial objects and appear to be detached portions of the Milky Way. They are actually satellite galaxies to our own large spiral galaxy.

Your Local Group of Galaxies: How to See Them

Galaxy	Distance (Light-years)	Constellation	Visibility
Milky Way	30,000 to center	Sagittarius	naked eye
Large Magellanic Cloud	160,000	Dorado	naked eye
Small Magellanic Cloud	205,000	Toucan	naked eye
IC 1613	240,000	Pisces	small telescope
Andromeda I dwarf	240,000	Andromeda	large telescope
Andromeda II dwarf	240,000	Andromeda	large telescope
Andromeda III dwarf	240,000	Andromeda	large telescope
Ursa Minor dwarf	245,000	Ursa Minor	—
Draco dwarf	260,000	Draco	—
Sculptor dwarf	280,000?	Sculptor	small telescope
Carina dwarf	300,000	Carina	—
Leo I	750,000	Leo	large amateur telescope
Leo II dwarf	750,000?	Leo	—
Fornax dwarf	800,000	Fornax	small telescope
Andromeda (M31)	2.5 million	Andromeda	naked eye
Triangulum Spiral (M33)	2.9 million	Triangulum	binoculars (naked eye for a few)
M110 (elliptical)	2.4 million	Andromeda	small telescope
M32 (elliptical)	2.4 million	Andromeda	small telescope
NGC 185 dwarf	2.4 million	Andromeda	small telescope
NGC 147 dwarf	2.4 million	Andromeda	large amateur telescope
LGS 3	2.4 million	Pisces	—

Besides portions of our own Milky Way, the next-brightest galaxy, visible from the northern hemisphere, is the Andromeda Galaxy (M31, or NGC 224). This is an immense spiral disk, similar to our Milky Way, and it is visible on clear dark nights as a small fuzzy spot in the constellation of Andromeda, north of the Great Square of Pegasus, the Horse. It is easy to miss this beautiful sky sight, but once it is spotted, with or without binoculars, it can always be found again. It is best seen during the months of September and October. Look to the southeast about an hour after twilight and find the Great Square of Pegasus, the Flying Horse. This is done by looking up at about 45 degrees (about halfway from the horizon to the zenith). Once Pegasus is found, use the upper left star of the Square, the second-magnitude star Alpheratz, which is also known as Alpha Andromedae, as your guide. Hold your fist at arm's length, palm tilted upward. Then extend your first three fingers; their width will be about 5 degrees. Five degrees to the left of Alpheratz are two dim stars. About 5 degrees farther are two more stars: Beta and Mu Andromedae. Just above these, about 5 degrees above the brightest one, is the dim patch of light that has been traveling through space for more than 2 million years from the Andromeda Galaxy.

The most difficult of the five galaxies to find with the unaided eye is the Triangulum Galaxy (M33, or NGC 598), in the western constellation Triangulum, the Triangle. The second-magnitude star Mirach (Beta Andromedae) is about midway between the Andromeda and Triangulum galaxies, about 7 degrees from each. To view Triangulum without optical aid is a challenge; sky conditions must be ideal: very dark skies away from all man-made lights. Only a few experienced professionals and enthusiastic amateur astronomers have ever seen it. A state or national park often provides the right conditions in which to view this distant object.

Although the combined visual magnitude of this object is listed at 6, which approximates the light of the dimmest stars to be seen by an observer, the Triangulum Galaxy is nearly invisible. The problem is that Triangulum is very large, about the size of our Moon in the sky. To get an idea of its size, hold

The great Andromeda Galaxy can also be seen with the naked eye, as a patch of fuzzy light that is about 2.2 million years old. These four exposures were 1, 5, 30, and 45 minutes long. The human eye sees much less than the 1-minute exposure. *Courtesy National Optical Astronomy Observatories.*

your little finger out at arm's length. This is roughly the size of this hard-to-see galaxy in the sky, equal to twice the diameter of the Moon or the Sun as it is seen by our eyes.

Cosmic Raindrops

The average distance between large galaxies like our Milky Way spiral is about 10 million light-years—a hundred of our galaxy's diameters. Think of a 1-inch (2.54-centimeter) disk, and another one 8.3 feet (2.5 meters) away, and you have the scale relationship. That the Milky Way and Andromeda galaxies are separated by only 2.2 million light-years is because they are close family members—condensed and sired from the same cosmic raindrops during the Big Bang storm.

The Great Leap Outward

Estimating cosmic distances of millions of light-years might appear like the height of egocentric folly, but astronomers have found an intelligent method to do so. They measure the periods of light fluctuations of a certain type of variable star known as the *Cepheid*. The brighter the Cepheid, the longer it will take to vary from bright to dim. This so-called *period-luminosity relationship* was first discovered by Henrietta Leavitt at Harvard University in 1908 and 1909. Cepheids are very bright white or yellow supergiants that pulse with periods of a few hours to fifty days. Their apparent brightness in our sky and their pulsations of light tell astronomers how bright they really are, which allows astronomers to estimate their distance away from Earth.

Over seven hundred Cepheids are known in our Milky Way, and several thousand of them have been found in nearby galaxies.

The Electromagnetic Spectrum

Electromagnetic radiation fills the Universe, but human eyes see only a minute part of it: visible light from blue-violet to red. This radiation is a flow of energy produced when electrically charged bodies such as electrons are propagated in a medium, such as air or space. Although its nature is not completely known, electromagnetic energy is understandable as either a wave or a stream of particles. As a wave, it has two properties: *wavelength,* the distance between peaks of the waves; and *frequency,* the number of waves per second. A sea about 3.3 feet (1 meter) high—the height of each wave from crest to trough—might have a wavelength of 30 feet (9.1 meters) and a frequency of .125 (each pulse lasting 8 seconds). To someone in a small boat, this might make for pleasant sailing. If this wave were electromagnetic radiation, it would be an ultralong wavelength, at the far red end of the spectrum.

Light radiation is usually measured in angstroms (about four billionths of an inch, one ten-billionth of a meter). Other units, such as millimeters, centimeters, and even kilometers are used for radio waves. Astronomers working in the range of infrared and radio radiation, which are longer wavelengths than visible light, often use the frequency of the radiation instead of its wavelength. They most often use *megahertz,* which is also how the FM radio band is defined. One hertz is 1 cycle, or wave, per second. One megahertz is 1 million cycles per second (1 million hertz).

Beyond our eyes' ability to see are the shorter-wavelength ultraviolet, X-ray, and the very high-energy gamma-ray radiations. In the other direction, toward the long wavelengths that are beyond the red end of visible light, are the infrared and the radio waves.

The frequency of the waves, or the number of oscillations per second, determines the energy of the wave. High-frequency radiation, such as gamma rays, is also high-energy radiation; low-frequency waves, such as long radio waves, are low-energy radiation.

Wavelengths of electromagnetic radiation can vary enormously. For example, the wavelength of a gamma ray is less than 0.1 nanometer, or one ten-billionth of a meter, but ordinary radio waves are many meters in length.

The Tramp Globular

Most of the 125 or so known globular clusters in our galaxy are found in a sphere, centered on the galactic core, with a diameter of 130,000 light-years. Their orbits, highly eccentric (elliptical, like an egg), move them around the Galaxy's core and through the galactic spiral disk once every 100 or 200 million years.

There are some exceptions, however, and the most well known is the distant globular cluster NGC 2419, in the constellation Lynx. It lies far beyond most of the other globulars and is often referred to as the "intergalactic tramp." NGC 2419 is 182,000 light-years from the Sun and 210,000 light-years from the Galaxy's center. This is over twice the Galaxy's diameter of 100,000 light-years, and the light reaching the Earth today from the cluster left almost two thousand centuries ago, about the time the human brain evolved to its present size with the appearance of *Homo sapiens*.

If NGC 2419 is indeed a gravitational member of our galaxy (some astronomers think it might be independent because of its great distance), it could take just 4.1 billion years to make one orbit around the center of the Galaxy.

None to a Million

Edmund Halley first mentioned a nebulous object in the constellation Hercules in 1715, just a year after he discovered it. Then, in 1764, the famous French astronomer Charles Messier observed it while pursuing his favorite pastime of hunting for comets. Messier described it as a "round and brilliant . . . nebula containing no stars." His short description dramatizes the great advances in optical and theoretical astronomy in the past two hundred years. He was very wrong, it turns out. The fact is that this so-called nebula, only rarely visible, as some fuzz, to the naked eye under ideal conditions, is now known to be one of the great globular star clusters that orbit our Galaxy—M13, which contains at least 1 million stars. This represents an astronomical leap in knowledge, from none to a million.

This globular cluster is also famous for a radio message that astronomers beamed to it in November 1974 from the large radio telescope at Arecibo, Puerto Rico. Because the cluster is some 25,000 light-years away from Earth, it will take the message 25,000 years just to reach its destination. Whether or not there are creature ears or instruments to receive it is a probability problem that can only be played with, not solved.

Typecasting Galaxies

The American astronomer Edwin P. Hubble, who revolutionized astronomy by giving the Universe a new time-and-distance scale, introduced a method of classification for galaxies in 1925. The basic system, although updated, is still in use today.

Hubble's classification system identifies three main types of galaxies: ellipticals, spirals, and barred spirals. The less frequently seen irregular galaxies were added later, and any galaxy with an absolute magnitude below −16 is considered a dwarf galaxy. The basic galactic types are further divided into subclasses, usually on the basis of their shape.

Elliptical galaxies are given the letter E followed by a number from 0 to 7, depending upon the flatness of the system. E0 galaxies, for example, are almost spherical in appearance, while E7 ones are practically flat. An example of an E6 elliptical in our Local Group of galaxies is NGC 205, which is one of the small satellite galaxies of Andromeda (M31).

Regular spiral galaxies have the basic pinwheel shape when they are viewed full on. Spirals are divided into three subgroups. Does the nucleus dominate? It is type Sa. Do the nucleus and arms share the honor? Then it is an Sb-type. Or do the galaxy's arms dominate? Then consider it an Sc-type spiral galaxy. The Triangulum Galaxy (M33) is a good example of an Sc spiral in the Local Group that has a low-profile nucleus.

Barred spiral galaxies (SB) have a distinct central bar, from the ends of which arms appear to be swirling. The Large Magellanic Cloud is today considered to be a barred spiral, even though it was viewed as an irregular galaxy for half a century.

Irregular galaxies (Irr) are generally subclassified accord-

The galactic zoo, like the life zoo on planet Earth, is filled with what seems like infinite variety. Edwin Hubble began the classification system for galaxies, which included the three main types shown here: elliptical, spiral, and barred spiral. Within each type, several subclasses are recognized, and other, minor types such as the irregulars and peculiars have been added. *Courtesy Mount Wilson and Las Campanas Observatories of the Carnegie Institution of Washington.*

ing to whether older, reddish (Population II) stars predominate or younger, blue (Population I) stars are dominant.

Each of these family groups in the galactic zoo may be observed with binoculars or a small telescope, but their structural details will be difficult to observe. Photographs, often with time exposures of several hours to collect the dim light, present much more detail than can the human eye. Many armchair amateurs are disappointed when they see these galaxies with the naked eye, because they have been spoiled with the beautiful, state-of-the-art images of deep space that the new technology has created and publishers have printed. But, given a night dark and clear, there is nothing like seeing the ancient light of faraway galaxies with your own eyes.

The Telltale Wake

The Magellanic Clouds, two satellite galaxies of our own Milky Way Galaxy, are visible only to observers south of the Earth's equator. There they shine, thirty-two times the area of the full Moon in the sky, luminous clouds of billions of stars. The Large Magellanic Cloud has a diameter of about 26,000 light-years (about one quarter the Galaxy's diameter), and the Small Magellanic Cloud has one of about 16,000 light-years (about half the Sun's distance from the galactic center). The Magellanic Clouds are the two closest galaxies to our spiral system (with the possible exception of a dwarf galaxy nicknamed Snickers) and are members of the so-called Local Group of galaxies. They are almost 200,000 light-years away (perhaps two galactic diameters) from our galaxy, in slightly different directions, and their centers are separated by about 80,000 light-years.

Twentieth-century astronomy has benefited immensely from their proximity to our own Solar System, about eleven times closer than the next sizable galaxy, famous Andromeda. Their closeness affords astronomers the best view they have of a great variety of astrophysical and astronomical processes, and new discoveries are often made. It has been speculated that the science of astronomy would have advanced much more rapidly over the past few centuries had the Magellanic Clouds been visible from the northern hemisphere.

Ragged around the edges, the Magellanic Clouds have been classified as irregular galaxies, since their shape is neither spiral nor elliptical, but a hint of spiral form has been observed in the Large Magellanic Cloud, which is now classified as a barred spiral. Both these small galaxies are gravitationally bound to our own galaxy, and many experts believe that they orbit one another every few billion years.

Radio astronomers have recently discovered a great trail of hydrogen, the Magellanic Stream, that may connect the two small galaxies to ours. Some experts believe this is a telltale wake, evidence that the orbits of the Magellanic Clouds take them through our galaxy's disk. If this is true, the hydrogen stream was probably drawn out from our galaxy during their last passage through the disk, perhaps 500,000 years ago, about the time when our hominid ancestors *Homo erectus* were beginning to stand upright.

A Magellanic Sampler

The Magellanic Clouds are so close to our Milky Way, by extragalactic standards, that many celestial objects discovered in our galaxy first have also been discovered and studied there—often from an advantageous perspective. Until the 1980s only one star-sized black hole was known, Cygnus X-1, although a number of other possible candidates existed. Then astronomers found a high-powered variable X-ray object in the Large Magellanic Cloud and designated it LMC X-3. Their observations showed that a main-sequence star was orbiting a dark, unseen companion about every 1.7 days. They believe that the mysterious object, with a mass somewhere between six and fourteen times our Sun, is the second stellar-sized black hole to pass the tough observational-data tests.

The first example of a rapidly rotating pulsar (neutron

The Large Magellanic Cloud, a "small" satellite galaxy seen from the southern hemisphere, orbits around our galaxy every few billion years. *Courtesy National Optical Astronomy Observatories.*

star) to be found outside our galaxy was discovered by Australian astronomers in 1983. This first extragalactic pulsar, designated PSR 0529-66, has what is considered an average rotation rate: once every 0.9571407 second.

Among the many star clusters and gaseous nebulae observed in the Large Magellanic Cloud, there are several supernova remnants flying through space. More than fifty of these expanding clouds, created by the gigantic, silent explosions of space, have been identified in this satellite galaxy. One of them, SNR 0519-69.0, is believed to be only five hundred years "old." It may have been seen on a clear night in the late-fifteenth century by someone in the southern hemisphere.

A Brilliant Million

At least 1 million of the Small Magellanic Cloud's 3 billion or so stars are brighter than Sirius—the brightest star in the Earth's sky. If 100,000 of them were situated 9 light-years away, roughly the distance of Sirius from our solar system, then nights on Earth would turn to dim, starlit days.

The Hungry Milky Way

The Large Magellanic Cloud will be slowly digested by our Milky Way Galaxy in the next few billion years. As the Cloud orbits around, or possibly through, the disk of our galaxy, it will gradually lose millions of its stars to the gravitational dominance of our spiral giant, which will in turn become larger and more powerful. Eventually it will attract the Small Magellanic Cloud and the satellite dwarf galaxies, those cosmic minnows that are still farther away, and digest them. Their capture will create new galactic tides and a season of fresh star formation in the Galaxy, which will have eaten its fill for the next several billion years. But there will never be such easy catches again—only the battle with Andromeda will remain.

The Infant Giants
of Magellan

There is very little intergalactic dust in the Magellanic galaxies when they are compared to our own Milky Way, but they make up for this deficiency with an excessive amount of hydrogen gas, from which new stars form. In the nebulous area of the Large Magellanic Cloud, named Constellation I by astronomer Harlow Shapley and numbered 1936 in the New General Catalogue, there is a large association of stars, with a mass equal to 24,000 Suns, not counting the vast gas clouds in which they are situated. Several hundred of these stars are blue-white giants, and many are newborns on the cosmic clock. Their location in the Large Magellanic Cloud gives astronomers a clear, unobstructed view into a busy stellar nursery. These infant blue giants formed only 20 million years ago, when the early apes of Earth roamed in large numbers what are now Kenya and Uganda.

The Great Tarantula

Within the Large Magellanic Cloud is a great gaseous nebula, larger and brighter than any other known in the Universe, variously called the Tarantula nebula, the Great Looped nebula, and 30 Doradūs, and designated NGC 2070

The Tarantula Nebula (also known as Dorado) is a great gas nebula in the Large Magellanic Cloud. It would be brighter than the full Moon even if it were 500 light-years from Earth. *Courtesy National Optical Astronomy Observatories.*

in the New General Catalogue. Under good viewing conditions from the southern hemisphere, this nebula can be seen by the unaided eye across a 190,000-light-year gulf of space and time.

The Tarantula's diameter is about 800 light-years, almost twenty-seven times larger than the great Orion nebula's diameter of 30 light-years. If Tarantula were in the position of the Orion nebula, it would fill the entire constellation of Orion and produce enough light to cast shadows on Earth. If it were within 500 light-years of the Earth, about the distance of the star Bellatrix, in Orion, it would fill half the Earth's sky, from the horizon to the zenith, with a diameter larger than that of two hundred full Moons. And even at that tremendous distance, it would be one third again as bright as the full Moon, 1.37 times as bright, to be precise.

The Hydrogen Bridge

The Large and Small Magellanic Clouds, separated from one another by about 80,000 light-years (four fifths the diameter of our galaxy), are rich in hydrogen gas. Estimates have put the amount of hydrogen in the Large Cloud as 10 percent of its mass (equal to 1 billion of its estimated mass of 10 billion Suns) and in the Small Cloud as high as 20 percent (equal to 400 million of its estimated mass of 2 billion Suns). Radio astronomy has also recently detected a hydrogen bridge, connecting the two satellite galaxies, which spans the full 80,000 light-years between them. This distance is more than 400,000 trillion times the length of the world's longest suspension bridge, the Verrazano Narrows, in New York City.

Far Starlight

The most distant object that can be seen without the help of a telescope or binoculars is the Triangulum Galaxy (M33). This light is the oldest we can see with our naked eyes.

The total light from the Triangulum Galaxy is estimated to be 3 billion times that of the Sun, plus or minus 20 percent.

Its surface brightness is so low that it is almost as dark as the background sky. Its distance and the slight obscuring effect of interstellar dust cause this.

The distance to this member of the Local Group of galaxies is about 2.3 million light-years (700 kiloparsecs or 700,000 parsecs). This is about 13.6 million trillion miles (21.8 million trillion kilometers) away.

The photons of light striking the eyes of a person observing the Triangulum Galaxy left their source 2.3 million years ago. On Earth, this would have been during the Pleistocene Epoch, when our early ancestors were perhaps looking up at incomparably darker skies and wondering what the dim and distant light they saw meant.

The question of a child, "How far can I see?" has its final answer in the galaxy of Triangulum.

The Open Arms in Triangulum

The Local Group has only one spiral galaxy in three with visibly open arms: M33 (NGC 598). Situated in the constellation Triangulum, not too far in the sky or in space from great Andromeda, this arms-spread spiral is perhaps 2.3 million light-years from Earth. When Edwin P. Hubble devised his classification system for galaxies, in the 1920s, there were three basic types of normal spirals: Sa, Sb, Sc. Spiral a designated a galaxy with a large nucleus and tightly wound spiral arms; spiral b meant a smaller nucleus and looser spiral arms; spiral c represented a galaxy with the smallest galactic nucleus and the most open arms. The Sc galaxy M33 is much smaller than Andromeda and the Milky Way, with a mass equal to about 15 billion Suns and a diameter approaching 60,000 light-years, but it takes up more apparent space in the sky than great Andromeda—a space equal to or slightly bigger than one full Moon—because it shows Earth its full-on face, even though its glow is dimmer. Bright Andromeda, however, gives us an almost edge-on view, tilted about 12 degrees, and the full face can never be seen from Earth. Because of M33's open arms, individual stars and other fea-

Two views of the local spiral galaxy with open arms, M33, in the constellation Triangulum, with its great hydrogen cloud, in the upper left of the full-view photograph, equal to the mass of 300 billion Earths. The second photograph is a close-up view of M33's central region, marbled with the procreative dust and gas lanes. This galaxy is an extremely challenging naked-eye galaxy, but dedicated amateur astronomers have seen it. *Courtesy National Optical Astronomy Observatories.*

tures can be resolved throughout the diffuse arms, and this has made optical studies of this spiral rewarding and productive. Blue-giant stars dominate the open arms and give a blue hue to the entire galaxy. M33 is rich in young stars and hydrogen-gas clouds. One great hydrogen cloud in its northwest corner is a full 1,000 light-years in diameter and contains material equal to the mass of 1 million Suns and over 300 billion Earths. It is as if the open arms in Triangulum had pitched out a gaseous ball.

The Slow Escape

A giant neighboring galaxy, hidden behind the clouds of gas and dust in the murky equatorial plane of our Milky Way, was discovered in 1968 by Paolo Maffei, an Italian astronomer. Designated Maffei 1, it was only the new technology of infrared astronomy, which can study radiations from deep space beyond the red end of the visible spectrum, that produced the discovery. It was not possible to detect the galaxy by its light, which is weakened by more than a factor of one hundred because of intervening dust and gas.

Maffei 1 is a giant elliptical galaxy with a mass 200 billion times that of the Sun, perhaps larger than our Milky Way Galaxy. It is about 4 million light-years away, at the edge of the Local Group of galaxies or just beyond. Maffei 1 is moving away from the Local Group at a velocity of 335,000 miles (540,000 kilometers) per hour and may eventually escape from the gravitational influence of the local galactic neighborhood, if it is a true member. At this speed, Maffei 1 is covering only 1 light-year every two thousand years, so its escape time will be slow indeed.

The Ancient Fuzz

Next September or October, on a clear moonless night when you are also away from city and rural lights, you can step outside, look to the northeast, and see something that is 2.2 million years old. There, southeast of Cassiopeia's well-known W, above the reddish star Mirach (Beta Andromedae), is the great Andromeda Galaxy, a fuzzy ellipse of ancient light that actually contains over 300 billion stars and is the largest galaxy in the Local Group, with a diameter estimated at some 130,000 light-years. Fuzzy Andromeda, also known as M31 and NGC 224, is 2.2 million light-years away, 13 million trillion miles (21 million trillion kilometers). When you see this fuzzy patch of light with your own eyes, contemplate the fact that this galactic glow from more than 300 billion stars left its source about the time the Colorado River began carving out the Grand Canyon and before there were any animals on Earth with brains large enough to wonder what it was.

The Little Cloud

The Andromeda Galaxy has probably been known for thousands of years. One of the first written records is from tenth-century Persia. Al Sufi, a Persian astronomer, wrote about it in A.D. 905 and described it as "the little cloud," an apt description when this galaxy is seen with human eyes. With binoculars, however, Andromeda's boundaries can be traced out to more than 4 degrees, which is eight times the diameter of the full Moon. Time-exposed photographs have enlarged its dimensions even more. Its true diameter is at least 130,000 light-years.

A little finger held at arm's length against the night sky equals about 1 degree, or twice the Moon's width. By moving your finger around the area of this ancient light, you will realize that this immense neighbor even makes a respectable showing in our sky from a distance of more than 2 million light-years.

The View from Andromeda

From a planet in one of the outer spiral arms of the Andromeda Galaxy, an observer could look across the 2.2-million-light-year cosmic gulf and barely discern our Milky Way Galaxy as a speck of fuzzy light. Our Sun (and Solar System) would be impossible to see, using the world's largest telescopes. Even if there were not the billions of brighter stars in our galaxy washing out the Sun's faint light, it would still be like trying to see a 60-watt light bulb at a distance of 5.1 million miles (8.2 million kilometers).

The Fifty-Year Growth Rate

Andromeda has played an important role in our understanding of the immense distances in the Universe. Before the 1920s, the true natures of the so-called spiral nebulae were not known. No one knew their true sizes and distances from Earth.

Then the Cepheids were discovered, bright variable stars that provided an astronomical yardstick for distant objects, including Andromeda. In December 1924, at a meeting of the American Astronomical Society, Edwin P. Hubble announced that he had used these variable Cepheids to solve the mystery of the spiral nebulae. They were not part of the Milky Way Galaxy, as many astronomers believed, but were separate "island universes" outside our galaxy.

Hubble's first distance for the Andromeda Galaxy was about 900,000 light-years. In the past sixty years, however, the distance has been corrected and increased to its current value of some 2.2 million light-years. As Andromeda's distance increased with improved measuring techniques, so too did its size—to about three times its earlier estimated diameter.

Distance estimates to faraway celestial objects such as Andromeda have been refined to the point that astronomers today have a reasonable certainty, within known limits, of the immense distances to our neighboring galaxies of the Local Group.

How Large Andromeda?

Andromeda is not only the nearest large galaxy to our Milky Way; it is also one of the largest and intrinsically brightest in the sky. Careful measurements of the density of the emulsion left on photographic negatives, using instruments

Three views of the great Andromeda Galaxy: a full view, a detail of its spiral arms and dust lane, and a detail of its central region. Andromeda, with its more than 300 billion stars, is as close to a twin to our Milky Way Galaxy as can be found in the Local Group. *Courtesy Mount Wilson and Las Campanas Observatories of the Carnegie Institution of Washington; and a Palomar Observatory Photograph. Courtesy California Institute of Technology.*

called densitometers, show that the galaxy may be as much as 180,000 light-years across, although the lower figure of 130,000 light-years is often used. But this is only the photographically detectable portion of the great spiral.

If Andromeda has an outer corona of dim, old stars proportionally as big as the Milky Way's, the system could be of truly gigantic size—much larger than the 1.5 Milky Way masses now considered a good estimate. This "weight" is now believed to be some 300 billion times that of our Sun, or 13,128,006[35] pounds (59,672,754[34] kilograms).

Galactic Bright

The Andromeda Galaxy shines across its gulf of 2.2 million light-years with a light equal to 30 billion times our Sun's.

Andromeda's Turnings

The great Andromeda Galaxy, like our galaxy, rotates about its axis, and the rotational velocity speeds up or slows down depending on the distance from the bright, elliptical nucleus. As the largest galaxy in the Local Group, with a total mass equal to 300 billion Suns, the stars and star stuff in some of the outermost regions of the spiral disk take the longest time of any local galaxy for a complete revolution. At a distance of 70,000 light-years from Andromeda's center, it will take a star 530 million years for a single circuit, over twice as long as our Sun and Solar System take to revolve around the hub of our galaxy. Just one of these Andromeda revolutions ago, a profusion of animals with external skeletons—for example, starfish and coral—were the dominant life forms on planet Earth. The Sun, Earth, and other planets were therefore born just eight Andromeda years ago.

A Diffuse Potential

There is enough gas, mostly hydrogen, in the Andromeda Galaxy to equal the mass of 6 million stars like our Sun and 54 billion planets similar to those in our solar system. If just one ninth of these planets were habitable like Earth, and at the same point in cosmic evolution, the total population of these planets would be 27 quintillion people.

Distant Sun

Our Sun is so brilliant that human eyes cannot even look directly at it. Astronomers give it an apparent visual magnitude (a measure of its brightness as observed from Earth) of -26.73. This compares to the full Moon (at -12) and to the brightest star in the sky, Sirius (at -1.5).

How bright would our life-giving star be if it were placed in the outer spiral arms of the great Andromeda Galaxy? Its visual magnitude would become $+29.1$, and even the most powerful telescopes on Earth would be unable to detect it. Even the Hubble Space Telescope would probably not be able to resolve it, because its ability to resolve 29th-magnitude stars is close to its design limits.

By moving the Sun to Andromeda, some 2.2 million light-years away, the difference in brightness would be a full fifty-six magnitudes. This means that its light as seen from planet Earth would be reduced more than 25 sextillion times.

Those Cosmic Clouds

Most galaxies in the Local Group contain large clouds of ionized hydrogen—the stuff of star birth. Astronomers call these HII regions. The beautiful, famous, and nearby Orion Nebula (M42) can even be glimpsed with the unaided eye on dark winter nights as the center fuzzy star in the sword of Orion, the Hunter. How does our own local Orion Nebula compare to other gaseous nebulae in our galactic neighborhood?

It seems a mere whiff. When the Orion cloud, estimated to be 30 light-years across, is compared to cloud NGC 604 of the Triangulum spiral galaxy, it turns out to be only one thirty-fifth its diameter. If this giant cloud were in the same location as the Orion Nebula, about 1,800 light-years away, it would be a great object in our sky, with a diameter seventy times that of our full Moon, and wash out all the light from our winter Milky Way. One fifth of the entire night sky would be filled with its swirling nebulosity, softly glowing from the light of the thousands of stars within it.

The Draco Dwarf

Probably the most common kind of galaxy in the Universe is the dwarf elliptical, of which there are several in the Local Group of galaxies. Because these dwarf systems are small and faint, they are extremely difficult to detect, and only the relatively nearby ones of the Local Group have been discovered, including the four found close to the Andromeda Galaxy in the early 1970s. The Draco dwarf system is just over 200,000 light-years away, twice our galaxy's diameter, and has a meager mass, equal to about 100,000 Suns. Its diameter is close to 3,200 light-years, which means that thirty of them could be lined up along the diameter of our Milky Way Galaxy. Even though the Draco dwarf is one of the smallest galaxies known, its diameter is still 2.5 million times larger than our Solar System's and 200 million times larger than the Sun-Earth distance.

The Shrinking Dwarfs

The dwarf elliptical galaxies in our Local Group—Sculptor, Fornax, Leo I, Leo II, Ursa Minor, Draco, and the recently discovered Carina—are old and dying star systems, because they lack the creative dust and gas from which new stars evolve. At present they are so thinly spread with stars (a thousand times sparser than the Sun's region of the Galaxy) that distant galaxies can be seen right through them.

Billions of years ago, this was not the case, but after the first star generations exploded and died, the resulting shock waves swept the gas and dust out of these small, gravitationally weak systems. Fewer and fewer new stars could be born. With the loss of this star seed, these dwarf galaxies grew smaller. Twelve or so billion years ago, for example, the

Draco dwarf galaxy probably was a hundred times more massive than now—with a mass equal to 10 million Suns, rather than 100,000. It appears that all the local dwarf galaxies are shrinking and in time will be absorbed by their giant neighbors.

The Sculptor Dwarf

This elliptical dwarf galaxy is a mere 280,000 light-years from our corner of the Milky Way. If it were much farther, our instruments would never be able to detect it.

If a normal-sized elliptical galaxy were brought to the same distance as the Sculptor group and 90 percent of its stars were removed, the dwarf and the giant would be almost indistinguishable. The mass of the Sculptor dwarf galaxy is about 3 million times that of the Sun. There is so little matter in this local dwarf that more distant stars and galaxies can be seen through it.

The Terminal Dwarf

The Ursa Minor dwarf galaxy has about the same mass as the Draco dwarf system—equal to 100,000 Suns—but its diameter of 7,800 light-years is more than twice Draco's, making it the local dwarf with the most widely spread out stars and therefore the weakest internal gravity.

While all nearby dwarf galaxies are the underdogs in a continual tidal battle with the dominant gravity of our Milky Way Galaxy, the Ursa Minor system is in the most immediate danger of tidal disruption. Astronomers predict that this dwarf already lies within the zone for tidal breakup and that its orbit is bringing it closer to the Milky Way Galaxy all the time. In fact, it may now be losing its border stars to our galaxy's gravity and will ultimately be torn apart completely, its stars becoming part of our galaxy's extended halo. So while all the local dwarfs are shrinking, some of them will soon be dying on our galaxy's gravitational rack, and Ursa Minor will be the first victim.

The Dusty Dwarf

A dwarf elliptical galaxy, NGC 185, is one of the Milky Way Galaxy's local neighbors, about the same distance away as Andromeda—2.2 million light-years—and considered one of its companions. Elliptical galaxies usually contain old stars and very little interstellar matter from which new stars can form, but NGC 185 is a rare exception. Within its small diameter of 9,800 light-years, toward the center, are two large

Three local elliptical dwarf galaxies, companions to Andromeda (NGC 205, NGC 147, and NGC 185). Probably the most common-type galaxy in the Universe, but the faraway ones cannot be observed. Dwarf galaxy NGC 185 is unusual in the amount of dust it contains—good for star birth. *Palomar Observatory Photographs, courtesy California Institute of Technology; and Yerkes Observatory.*

dust clouds, each about 100 light-years across, which are probably associated with a nearby cluster of blue-giant stars. Usually the dust in these interstellar clouds is very rarefied. Even if the thickness of the dust cloud is many times the diameter of our Solar System, it still would present less obstruction to light passing through it than does a thin layer of dust on a windowpane.

The Local Dwarf
That Did a Lot

A small irregular nebulous glow in the constellation Sagittarius, discovered by the American astronomer E. E. Barnard in the 1880s, became a breakthrough object for modern astronomy when Edwin P. Hubble carefully studied it during the early 1920s with the 60- and 100-inch telescopes at Mount Wilson.

After studying the nearby gaseous nebulae in our galaxy for two years, which trained his eyes and mind for the much fainter objects that were his ultimate goal, objects at the center of a great scientific debate—Were these nebulae composed of gas or stars? Were they in the Galaxy or outside it?— Hubble then went on to an unspectacular dwarf nebula, NGC 6822, to study it thoroughly and photograph it over the next two years.

Fifty long-exposure photographs of NGC 6822 were taken over this time, and Hubble patiently found eleven Cepheid variable stars on the plates. It was obviously not a gaseous nebula, but a cloud of stars. Then, using the known relationship between their periods and brightnesses, Hubble measured NGC 6822's distance. He placed it the better part of 1 million light-years away (even though it turned out to be farther)—the greatest distance that astronomers had ever measured. This local dwarf became the first celestial object known to lie outside the Milky Way galactic system. It would lead to the great Andromeda and then beyond, measuring the way to the distant galaxies, their recession, and finally the theory of the expanding Universe. All this, thanks to a local dwarf.

A Cosmic Mating

Recent theories of galaxy formation and evolution, an intense and wide-open area of current research, suggest that well-formed spiral galaxies could merge and form elliptical galaxies or that the largest galaxies in dense clusters could cannibalize their smaller neighbors and grow even larger. These theories, and variations on them, are supported by observations of peculiar galactic systems that show severe disruptions because of tidal interactions, as well as the giant galaxies at the centers of galaxy clusters that have more than one nucleus. Most galaxies, then, may have evolved by a gradual accumulation process—through an accretion of smaller star systems or diffuse gases.

We may finally come to know for certain that galaxies are heavily influenced—indeed, often shaped—by their neighbors, the close stellar systems with which they interact. It has even been speculated that all the twenty-five or more galaxies in the Local Group may, in some distant time, merge together and become a supergiant galaxy. Our own galaxy may collide with Andromeda in another 10 billion years or so. Such a cosmic mating would produce a new burst of star formation and all that come with it—including planets and life.

Weight Gain of the Local Group

New observations by radio astronomers suggest that our galaxy may be accreting matter—in other words, gaining "weight"—at the rate of 0.2 solar mass a year—an amount equal to about 66,590 Earths. Astronomers at the American National Radio Astronomy Observatory's 140-foot (43-meter) antenna have recently observed high-speed clouds of hydrogen moving toward the galactic center, clouds from many positions around our Milky Way Galaxy. When they observed in the direction of the constellation Sagittarius, the Archer, toward the center of the Galaxy, most clouds were approaching, evidently from the other side. When their antennas were turned away from the Galaxy's center, all clouds were still rushing toward the telescope. The few hydrogen clouds that appeared to be moving in the wrong direction, away from the observers when they looked toward the Galaxy's center, have probably already fallen past us and are dropping inward, toward the center.

Where is this matter coming from? It could be coming from the gulfs between the galaxies; or it could be stolen from our neighbors. Theft may be likely, considering the fact that our Milky Way Galaxy is one of the two largest galaxies in the Local Group.

Over a period of 1 million years, matter sufficient to create 200,000 stars the size of the Sun will apparently be captured by our Milky Way. This at first seems to be a huge amount of matter, until the Galaxy's total weight is considered: as much as 1 trillion Suns. In 1 million years our Milky Way will gain only one ten-millionth of its own weight.

By the time the Sun dies, maybe 5 billion years from now, our galaxy will have increased its weight by only 0.001 its current weight, or one tenth of 1 percent. If a 200-pound (91-kilogram) person gained the same proportion of weight, it would be an increase of about 3 ounces (85 grams), hardly enough to move the bathroom scale.

Galactic Softball

A red giant star has been found in the constellation Libra, the Scales, that may be the most distant star in our Milky Way. Another possible explanation is that it may have been somehow hit our way by one of our satellite galaxies, the Small or the Large Magellanic Cloud.

When astronomers were searching for new X-ray objects in the sky with the *Einstein X-ray Observatory* satellite, they discovered a dim, 18th-magnitude star that appeared to be an immense supergiant star at a great distance. The star is estimated at a distance of about 400,000 light-years, some four times the estimated diameter of our Milky Way's disk. The astronomers speculate that this star may have been ejected from one of our neighbors and is very weakly bound to the Milky Way. Further study of this curious star may help us learn more about the actual mass of our galaxy's distant outer halo. In the meantime, this unusual star appears to be the first known example of a galactic pop foul.

CHAPTER 3

THE FARAWAY
GALAXIES

"And beyond our galaxy are other galaxies, in the universe all told at least a hundred billion, each containing a hundred billion stars. Do these figures mean anything to you?"

—John Updike, *The Centaur*

Galaxies You Can't See

The next time you see the bowl of the Big Dipper, contemplate the fact that there are at least 1 million galaxies between the four stars that outline the bowl. Indeed, if you stretch out your arm, clench your fist, and point it anywhere in the night sky, your fist will cover an area that contains about 1 million galaxies in the depths of space and time. Except for the five naked-eye galaxies mentioned in Chapter 2, all of them are invisible to the human eye. Only the largest telescopes on Earth or in orbit can bring the other thousands of distant galaxies to the human eye. In essence, these faraway galaxies were discovered by the human mind.

Galactic Groupies

As a cosmic rule, galaxies are found in groups that contain anywhere from two to thousands of members. Our Local

Group, of about two dozen members, is not unusual. Beyond our local neighborhood, four other "nearby" galactic groups have been discovered and charted. They are the Sculptor Group (also called the South Galactic Pole Group); the M81 Group, in the constellation Ursa Major; the Leo Group, in the constellation by the same name; and the M101 Group, also in Ursa Major.

Astronomers believe that the closest of these groups is that of M81. It contains four main galaxies and perhaps eight others, at a distance of about 7 million light-years from the Milky Way. The members include the two great spirals M81 and M82; the peculiars NGC 3077 and NGC 2976; and the irregular systems Ho II, NGC 2366, and IC 2574. The last two irregulars are similar in appearance to our Magellanic

A computer photomap (negative print) of the 1 million brightest galaxies as seen from the Earth's northern hemisphere. The faintest galaxies on the map are 160,000 times dimmer than can be seen with the unaided eye. *Courtesy M. Seldner, Edward J. Broth, and P. J. E. Peebles, Princeton University.*

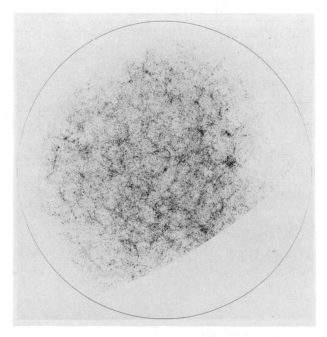

Clouds. Another possible member of this group is the galaxy NGC 2366, in the constellation Camelopardalis, the Giraffe. This galaxy is situated about 14 degrees away from the cluster's center in the sky. NGC 2976 is a tiny dwarf, with a diameter of only 2,000 light-years, about one twentieth that of our Large Magellanic Cloud. NGC 2403 can be seen through binoculars as a large hazy spot; it resembles our Local Group's M33, the so-called Pinwheel Galaxy.

The Sculptor Group is at an estimated distance of between 7.8 and 9.8 million light-years. Sculptor contains at least six galaxies. The unusual-looking galaxy NGC 55, which could be either a spiral or an irregular, is believed to be one of the closest galaxies to our Local Group. Some astronomers think it resembles one of the Magellanic Clouds or is an unusual spiral that is seen edge on. Its mass is estimated at about 46 billion Suns, and its brightness is calculated at some 6 billion times that of our Sun, which makes it one of the brightest galaxies in the southern sky. Other galaxies in the Sculptor Group are NGC 253; NGC 300; NGC 7749; NGC 247, in the constellation Cetus, the Whale; and perhaps NGC 45. While it is very likely that small and dim elliptical or irregular galaxies are group members, they are invisible to our present-day instruments.

The Leo Group, in the constellation by the same name, contains four galaxies that can all be seen through small, amateur-sized telescopes. They were all discovered and first catalogued in the eighteenth century by the famous French astronomer Charles Messier. The three spirals (M65, NGC 3623; M66, NGC 3627; and M96, NGC 3368) and one elliptical (M105, NGC 3379) appear to be accompanied by a number of dim galaxies. The Leo Group is estimated to be at a distance of 29–38 million light-years from us at the near edge of what is known as the Virgo Cloud, an immense mass of thousands of galaxies.

Another small cluster of distant galaxies is the M101 Group, in Ursa Major. The main galaxy in this group is the beautiful spiral M101 (NGC 5457), one of the bluest galaxies known. Its brightness comes from large numbers of young, hot, blue stars in its arms. The diameter of M101 has been estimated at about 90,000 light-years. Other galaxies in the M101 group are NGC 5477, NGC 5485, and at least eight smaller members, all of which are estimated at a distance of about 15 million light-years.

The Cosmic Biggies

Galaxies are the largest individual structures in the Universe. Their average diameter has been put at about one half that of our own Milky Way Galaxy—some 50,000 light-years. The average brightness of a galaxy has been estimated at 50 billion Suns, again about half the traditional value given to our galaxy.

Brightness comparisons to the Milky Way are *very* tentative, however, because we are locked in our little cosmic corner within the Galaxy and cannot be certain of how much light our great spiral sends across the intergalactic gulfs. The mass of a typical large galaxy may be about 1 trillion times that of the Sun. Taking into account the growing estimates on the mass of our own Milky Way based on possible matter in its outer halo regions, our galaxy's mass could be as much as one to two times the 1-trillion-Sun figure.

What You See Is
Not What You Get

Are the types of galaxies observed in the nearby galactic groups representative of the rest of the Universe? Astronomy has learned that, just as distant dim stars can escape our instruments, so can the dim and distant galaxies.

According to a survey of the thousand brightest galaxies listed in the Revised Shapley Ames Catalog of galaxies, 75 percent of them are spirals, 20 percent are ellipticals, and about 5 percent are irregulars. When their distances are taken into account, however, the distribution picture changes. If the volume of space sampled is limited, then

These galaxies are members of other "close" groups beyond our Milky Way's Local Group. The large spiral galaxy NGC 253, in the southern hemisphere's Sculptor group; galaxies M81 and M82, in an Ursa Major group; and spiral galaxy M101, in another Ursa Major group. Galaxies are not found alone in the Universe. *Courtesy The Anglo-Australian Observatory, © 1979; and Hale Observatories.*

fainter galaxies are found more frequently: 30 percent are spirals; 60 percent are ellipticals, many of them small and dim; and 10 percent are irregulars. At great distances, the small ellipticals probably hide under the aprons of their dominant parent galaxies. Closer to home, astronomers see them clustered about the larger spirals such as Andromeda (M31), in our Local Group.

Windmills in the Sky

How galaxies appear depends on what instruments are used to observe them. Photographic, electronic, radio, infrared, ultraviolet, and X-ray observations will create very different images of the same celestial object. Early photographs of the spiral galaxy M65 (NGC 3623), in the constellation Leo, taken in 1888, resembled a windmill. The arms of this galaxy looked like four huge windsails. Later photographs, taken with more sophisticated photographic materials and larger telescopes, depict a more typical spiral galaxy, with a smooth system of coil-like arms and a narrow lane of dust on the nearer edge. This galaxy and two nearby large spirals—NGC 3627 (M66) and NGC 3628—form a small group about 34 million light-years away. The two brighter galaxies (M65 and M66) are separated by a distance of about 180,000 light-years.

Distant Galactic Light in Your Binoculars

A good pair of standard 7×50 binoculars will allow viewing of about two dozen distant galaxies beyond our Local Group. Ten of the brightest, all spirals except the elliptical galaxy M49, are listed here for observers in the northern hemisphere. These galaxies range in brightness from one half to one tenth the brightness of the dimmest naked-eye star. When we consider the time this galactic starlight has taken to reach the Earth (equal to its distance in light-years), we are talking about millions and tens of millions of years. The last galaxy (M104) on the list emitted its light long before humankind inhabited planet Earth and at a geological time when Antarctica and Australia may have been one supercontinent.

These two spiral galaxies are among several that can be seen by the amateur astronomer with a pair of good binoculars. NGC 2403, in Camelopardalis, is some 8 million light-years away; and NGC 4826, in Coma Berenices (also known as the "Black-Eye Galaxy"), is about 25 million light-years away. A Palomar Observatory Photograph, *courtesy California Institute of Technology; and courtesy Mount Wilson and Las Campanas Observatories of the Carnegie Institution of Washington.*

GALAXIES THROUGH BINOCULARS

Galaxy	Constellation	Best Seen	Approx. Age of Light and Distance
M81 (NGC 3031)	Ursa Major	Spring–Summer	7 million years
NGC 253	Sculptor	Autumn	8 million years
NGC 2403	Camelopardalis	Autumn–Spring	8 million years
M94 (NGC 4736)	Canes Venatici	Spring–Summer	20 million years
M64 (NGC 4826)	Coma Berenices	Spring–Summer	25 million years
M65 (NGC 3623)	Leo	Spring	30 million years
M66 (NGC 3627)	Leo	Spring	30 million years
M51 (NGC 5194)	Canes Venatici	Spring–Summer	35 million years
M49 (NGC 4472)	Virgo	Spring	40 million years
M104 (NGC 4594)	Virgo	Spring	40 million years

Out-of-Gas Ellipticals?

Astronomers traditionally believed that elliptical galaxies contain little gas and dust, because little or none was observed. But that view has changed dramatically in the past few years. In 1985, astronomers using the *Einstein X-Ray Observatory* satellite announced finding hot gas in the coronas of more than fifty elliptical galaxies. The temperature of the gas was measured at about 10 million degrees Celsius (18 million degrees Fahrenheit).

How did this gas get into the galactic outback? The experts argue that powerful supernova explosions expelled it from the central regions. How much? The estimated mass of each of the galaxies' coronas studied was some 1 billion Suns, not enough to drastically revise the mass of a particular galaxy or to find a large portion of what astronomers consider the missing mass of the Universe. One such galaxy, for example, M86, in the constellation Virgo, had an estimated mass of 130 billion times the mass of the Sun, and so the discovery of the corona gas and its mass increased its weight by less than 1 percent.

For decades, astronomers wondered where the gas and other matter went after star explosions in elliptical galaxies. Now they know that the ellipticals are not out of gas after all.

Mysterious Galaxy M82

Galaxy M82 (NGC 3034), in constellation Ursa Major, is a peculiar cosmic object. Compared to its nearby neighbor, roundish and aesthetic M81 (NGC 3031), it is a pencil-thin streak of dim glow through the eyepiece of a small telescope. Amateur astronomers often enjoy looking for M82's dark band, which crosses the center of this edge-on irregular galaxy. A glimpse of this band can sometimes be caught by people with sharp eyes who use a telescope under velvet black skies.

The dark lane in M82 has puzzled astronomers for years. Is this a galaxy undergoing a violent event? Is it an exploding galaxy? No one is sure, but new evidence suggests a more mundane but complicated reality.

M81 and M82 are probably the central members of a small group of galaxies in Ursa Major. This galactic relationship is not unlike our own Milky Way and nearby Andromeda, the two main members of the Local Group. In fact, so-called twin spiral galaxies such as these have been observed in large numbers and have always been an astronomical curiosity that compels a question: Why are there so many twin spirals sharing space and time together? The distance to M82 is estimated at about 10 million light-years. This puts it between four and five times the distance to our next-door neighbor Andromeda.

Starting in the 1960s, M82 was placed in the growing group of radio galaxies and was designated 3C 231 (its listing as object number 231 in the Third Cambridge Catalog of radio sources). Its radio energy, however, was just barely detectable by the radio survey telescope then being used. Meanwhile, some astronomers observing in visual light with optical telescopes found that its light was polarized, perhaps because the galaxy was surrounded by large clouds of dust.

A ragged, violent galaxy (M82) and a smooth spiral (M81) are sharply contrasting galactic neighbors. The center of M82 may have exploded 1.5 million years ago, while M81 appears a calm cosmic carousel with a mass of about 250 billion Suns. A Palomar Observatory Photograph, *courtesy California Institute of Technology;* and a Lick Observatory Photograph, *Courtesy Lick Observatory.*

Galaxy M82 also appeared to have material streaming out from its center at more than 600 miles per second (1,000 kilometers per second) in one direction and 660 miles per second (1,062 kilometers per second) in another. Did this result from a violent event in the galaxy's center? A faint ring of material observed around its companion galaxy, M81, was thought to be further proof of a big galactic boom.

The belief that M82 was exploding has now been tempered by two decades of additional observation. First, near-infrared photographs of the galaxy's center show that huge, bright hydrogen clouds, similar to the Orion Nebula (M42), in the Milky Way, are present. Deep in the galaxy's dusty center, the long-wave-infrared viewing showed mobs of powerful bright and bluish O and B stars. These were burning fiercely all along but could not be seen in visual light because of surrounding thick dust. It is now considered likely that runaway star formation has recently occurred, and it could be this activity, not a violent explosion, that is causing M82 to be bright and active in the radio wavelengths. Then too, it could have been a violent explosion at its center that began all the new star births.

More recent observations of the streams of matter flowing from this spiral now suggest that the galaxy's rotation is what astronomers are observing. The 60-mile (100-kilometer) per-second difference in the two streams of matter might just be due to the fact that one is spinning toward the line of sight of our telescopes and the other is spinning away, similar to what is happening in our Milky Way.

The polarized light was another matter. The process of polarization is not completely understood, because the nature of light is not completely understood. Polarization can be caused by light being reflected from elongated particles of dust—dust grains oriented in certain directions by weak magnetic fields. A partial polarization such as this is observed in the interstellar medium. In fact, polarization of sunlight from the dust tail of a comet is what gives these celestial vagabonds their beautiful featherlike luminescence in the sky. Strong polarization of the 10-million-year-old light of

M82 all the way out to the shell of dust surrounding the galaxy suggests that it results from reflection and not some more explosive process.

The consensus today is that the experts were fooled for years by the vast, swirling dust clouds, which acted as mirrors. What was once thought to be a violently exploding galaxy is now just a very dusty one playing tricks with light.

Great Orions

The mysterious innards of spiral galaxy M82 may be caused by thousands of large gas clouds—enough to equal 100,000 of our own beautiful Orion Nebula. This is the conclusion of astronomers at the University of California at San Diego who have used the 200-inch (5-meter) telescope at Palomar Mountain to study the galaxy closely.

Our local, green-tinted Orion Nebula can be seen with the unaided eye from Earth. If we were to have thousands of huge nebulae like it near us in the Galaxy, the night sky would be a striking display of brightly glowing streaks and clouds illuminated by the light of tens of thousands of hot, bright stars. What explanations might our ancestors have found for the appearance of such a beautifully swirling night sky?

The Ragged Galaxy

Distorted and ragged-looking, galaxy M82 (NGC 3034) lies in Ursa Major at a distance of about 10 million light-years. Even at this distance, this peculiar, spindle-shaped galaxy is the second-"brightest" in the sky after our galaxy when seen through infrared telescopes, in the nonoptical portion of the spectrum. The reason for this is that huge clusters of extremely hot stars, containing up to ten thousand each, are heating up large amounts of the gas and dust to high temperatures, which radiate in the infrared. "High" in this case means −170 degrees Celsius (−274 degrees Fahrenheit), as compared to more "normal," interstellar temperatures of −270 degrees Celsius (−454 degrees Fahrenheit). This warm dust and gas radiates 50 million times more energy than does our Sun. Such a tremendous energy output, however, is dwarfed by the colossal power of a mysterious event that *may have caused* (no one is certain) the large and hot star clusters in the first place: a violent explosion in the center of the galaxy about 1.5 million years ago, which sent out a mass of expanding material equal to as much as 5 million Suns. The debris—composed of gas and dust filaments—is flying outward at over 2 million miles (3.2 million kilometers) per hour and is responsible for the distorted and ragged shape of M82. If there ever were life forms in the central region of this galaxy, they are all extinct now.

Dense in a Sense

One of the most beautiful spiral galaxies in the sky is M81 (NGC 3031), which lies in the constellation Ursa Major at a distance of about 7 million light-years. With its spiral arms moderately close to its sides, M81's lovely symmetry is in sharp contrast to its disturbed and ragged-looking neighbor M82.

Traditionally known as Bode's nebula, since it was discovered by the German astronomer Johann Bode in 1774, M81 has smaller dimensions than our galaxy or Andromeda —about 36,000 light-years—and an actual brightness equal to some 20 billion Suns.

Besides its beauty, M81 has another claim to fame: it is one of the densest galaxies known. Even though its dimensions are considerably smaller than the Milky Way and Andromeda, its mass, of about 250 billion Suns, exceeds our galaxy's, and its density may be twice as great as Andromeda's. Even so, its stars are separated on the average by about 6 light-years, so if a typical star diameter in M81 is represented by 1 inch (2.54 centimeters), then the next star would be 147 miles (236.5 kilometers) away—hardly overcrowded conditions from the human perspective, but still dense in a galactic sense.

Long Exposure

Toward the end of the 1920s, when the Mount Wilson 100-inch (2.5-meter) telescope was operational, Milton L. Humason began obtaining information on the velocities of the most distant galaxies. He did this by recording and analyzing the spectral red shift*—a shift toward the red end of the spectrum, to longer wavelengths, which tells astronomers that the object is moving away from the point of observation, Earth. Study of an object's red shift can tell astronomers much about a particular galaxy, including its velocity of recession and its distance. Humason, in 1935, found a galaxy in an Ursa Major cluster of galaxies that was speeding away from the Milky Way at 94 million miles (151 million kilometers) an hour. Some of the distant galaxies that Humason observed were so faint that the exposure times on the photographic plates sometimes lasted for ten nights or more!

WHAT IS THE RED SHIFT?

* A spectrograph is an instrument for photographing the spectra of electromagnetic radiation, including visible light. The dark spectral lines from the light of a receding object are shifted to the longer wavelengths, toward the red end of the spectrum (red light has the longest wavelength of all the colors). This is known as the red shift, and indicates motion away from the observer. Just the opposite is true if the object is moving toward the observer: the wavelengths are compressed, and a blue shift is seen.

The higher the red shift of a cosmic object, the farther away it is in space and time and the higher its recession velocity in the expanding Universe. Quasars have the highest red shifts recorded. Red shifts are essential, along with the value of the Hubble constant, in determining velocities and distances of faraway cosmic objects. This in turn allows astronomers to estimate the age, the expansion rate, and the ultimate fate of the Universe.

A Supergiant Spiral

Some 230 million light-years away, in the extended Perseus supercluster of galaxies, is the largest spiral galaxy ever discovered. Designated UGC 2885, in the Uppsala General Catalogue of galaxies in the northern hemisphere, it is receding from the Local Group of galaxies at 13.4 million miles (21.6 million kilometers) per hour. Its mass is estimated at 2 trillion times that of our Sun, over twenty times the estimate for our entire galaxy.

This supergiant two-armed spiral galaxy has a diameter of at least 815,000 light-years, a full eight times larger than that of the Milky Way. Halfway out from its nucleus, stars and gas clouds revolve around the hub once every 2 billion years —not more than ten times since the beginning of the Universe.

If a starship were to circumnavigate the outer spiral arms of UGC 2885 at one hundredth the speed of light, which is almost 122,000 times faster than the U.S. speed limit of 55 miles (88 kilometers) per hour, it would take about 256 million years to complete the voyage. If this supergiant spiral were about 1.1 million light-years away from the Earth, in between our galaxy and Andromeda, positioned full on with its arms spread open, its trillions of stars would fill an arc of sky over 40 degrees across, having a diameter of almost 100 full Moons in the night sky. The same would be true for an unknown planet's sky in the outer arms of the Andromeda Galaxy. The supergiant's gravity would dominate the Local

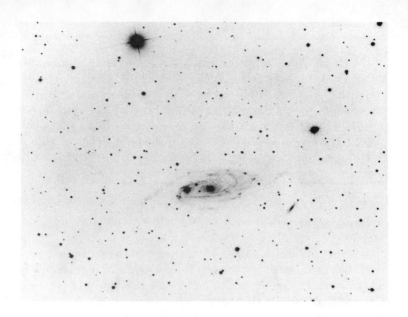

One of the largest spiral galaxies known in the Universe, supergiant UGC 2885, has a diameter of at least 800,000 light-years—eight times that of our Milky Way. *Courtesy Bruce W. Carney and National Optical Astronomy Observatories.*

Group and might in time cannibalize the Milky Way and Andromeda, becoming in the process an even larger supergiant galaxy.

Cosmic Bridges

Some galaxies that are fairly distant from one another have actual intergalactic bridges connecting them, made of the same stuff the galaxies are composed of: stars and nebulae. These intergalactic bridges often reach lengths of 200,000 light-years, twice the diameter of our galaxy. No toll has yet been established.

Common Galaxies

Elliptical galaxies—dwarf, average, giant, and supergiant—are the most common galaxies in the Universe and are in the majority. They are the smallest (often only 3,000 light-years in diameter) and the largest (as much as 300,000 light-years in diameter) and often contain a minimum of interstellar matter in their central regions. Some of the dwarfs are known to have masses equal to about 100,000 Suns, while the supergiant ellipticals may contain masses equal to 10 trillion Suns—the largest and most massive single bodies known to exist in the Universe.

While elliptical galaxies are in the majority, they have neither the youth nor the beauty of the spirals. And for those without the interstellar dust and gas, their star-bearing years are over. They are the senior citizens of today's Universe.

Hats Off to the Sombrero

The edge-on view of the Sombrero Galaxy (M104, NGC 4594), in Virgo, is not just a beautiful sight to behold in long-exposure photographs, with its huge, brilliant nucleus and its dark, distinct lane of equatorial dust; it also holds an important place in the history of modern astronomy and the discovery of the expanding Universe.

American astronomer Vesto Melvin Slipher, of Lowell Observatory, was measuring line-of-sight velocities of the controversial "nebulae" in 1912, years before they were known to be great island universes external to our own galactic system, rather than clouds of gas within our Milky Way. In a two-year period, Slipher compiled a list of velocities of fifteen "nebulae" (galaxies) by studying their spectral lines; all but two of them, later determined to be local galaxies, were moving away from our Solar System.

Sombrero had the speed record among these galaxies—its red shift (speed of recession measured by increased wavelengths) told Slipher it was receding at 2.5 million miles (4 million kilometers) per hour. This was the highest speed known to exist at that time, and it was strong evidence that Sombrero and other "nebulae" were not just local gas clouds. Edwin Hubble would use the Sombrero and other "nebulae"

The Sombrero Galaxy (M104), in Virgo, was the fastest-receding galaxy known during the first few decades of the twentieth century: 2.5 million miles (4 million kilometers) per hour. Today it is considered slow by cosmic standards. A Palomar Observatory Photograph. *Courtesy California Institute of Technology.*

velocities as a launchpad for his historic astronomical journey that would discover the Earth, Solar System, and Galaxy in an expanding Universe.

Today, the Sombrero's amazing recession speed of millions of miles each hour is far below the known cosmic speed limits. The Hydra cluster of galaxies, at 3.3 billion light-years —hardly the most distant objects known—is speeding away from us fifty-four times faster than Sombrero, which is like comparing a Model T put-putting along at 15 miles (24 kilometers) per hour to the world land-speed record set at Bonneville Salt Flats in a rocket-powered craft at close to 800 miles (1,300 kilometers) per hour. But Sombrero was the first of the fastest, and it is still beautiful to behold. Hats off, everyone.

The Whirlpool's Illusion

One of the most famous galaxies in the cosmic realm is the Whirlpool Galaxy (M51, NGC 5194), in the constellation Canes Venatici at a distance of about 37 million light-years. In 1845 Lord Rosse, of Ireland, observed that it had a spiral pattern—the first time this shape was ever observed. Because no one in the 1880s knew external galaxies existed,

The famous Whirlpool Galaxy (M51) is having a gravitational romance with a smaller galaxy that orbits around it. A Palomar Observatory Photograph. *Courtesy California Institute of Technology.*

many astronomers of the day thought it might be a "solar system" in formation; their scale was off by millions.

Besides its historical and popular importance, what separates the Whirlpool from any other face-on-view spirals is its association with a smaller irregular or elliptical galaxy, NGC 5195. The two are having a gravitational romance, a relationship that has lasted for hundreds of millions of years. The smaller galaxy is slightly nearer to us than M51, orbits around it, has completed its pass in front, and will pass behind it millions of years from now. Along the way, one of M51's spiral arms appears to have reached out and touched the smaller galaxy. Computer simulations indicate, however, that this physical connection is an illusion produced because the objects lie in the line of sight.

This is not to say that there are not real tidal distortions between M51 and NGC 5195 (indeed, many stars from the outer, extended arm of M51 will follow the smaller galaxy into intergalactic space), only that their physical contact is an optical illusion. This need not take away from their real gravitational romance.

Two Peculiars with Tidal Tails

Every good-sized crowd of people has its eccentric or peculiar individuals, and the same is true of galaxies. About 1–2 percent of all galaxies are unusual enough to be called peculiar by astronomers, and about one fifth of this number are considered odd because of the way they interact with their neighbors.

Two peculiar galaxies, NGC 4038 and 4039, lying in the small southern constellation Corvus at a distance of about 50 million light-years, are having a gravitational fight over their territory, and both are getting mangled in the process. More commonly known as the Antennae (and sometimes the Ring-Tail Galaxy), they have been struggling for about 800 million years, according to computer models. The peculiar twosome

These two galaxies, NGC 4038 and 4039, are having a gravitational tug-of-war. They are also known as the Antennae, because of large tidal tails, barely visible in optical light, that stream out into far space as a result of their cosmic battle. A Palomar Observatory Photograph. *Courtesy California Institute of Technology.*

are orbiting each other as well as rotating on their own axes, which makes for galactic upset and heartburn in their cores; as a result, both lack normal nuclei. During their gravitational war, these galaxies have shot out long tails that look like drooping bunny ears—thus their common name, Antennae. The Antennae are composed of the galaxies' outlying stars and gas and arch out for 100,000 light-years, the diameter of our entire galaxy. The hydrogen gas alone could produce 1.5 billion stars as large as the Sun.

How long did it take for the galaxies to grow their long tidal tails during this close encounter? Advanced astronomers elsewhere in the Galaxy probably could have seen them beginning to grow about 500 million years ago, when glaciers on the Earth were active in what is now the Sahara Desert and when the most advanced life-forms were about on the level of the sea urchin.

Cosmic Collisions

Ring galaxies are very rare and peculiar star systems that have holes punched in their centers. A few of these strange objects have been found, usually in the shape of an elliptical ring; their centers either have no luminous material at all or sometimes a bright off-center nucleus.

Computer simulation models support the belief that ring galaxies are the result of head-on collisions between two galaxies. The central region of the more passive galaxy is ejected as the other galaxy storms through it, and an expanding ring of stars is formed in its outer region, composed of countless new hot stars and gases that form from the ejected central mass.

The Cartwheel Galaxy, about 500 million light-years away in Sculptor, is an example of a ring galaxy; its diameter is 170,000 light-years. Hundreds of millions of years ago, a smaller galaxy went right through its center; astronomers have located this galaxy about 250,000 light-years from the Cartwheel, it having long since left the scene of the trespass.

Ring galaxies are the result of head-on collisions between two galaxies, in which one punches a hole right through the other. *Courtesy National Optical Astronomy Observatories.*

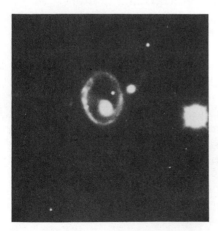

Amazingly, when galaxies pass through other galaxies there are few, if any, "short-term" cataclysmic events like supernova chain reactions or millions of stellar collisions. The vast distances between stars prevent this. What takes place is more like a slow splash pattern created by the warring gravities, which ejects the stars and star stuff into the outer regions, where the ring forms. The Cartwheel Galaxy's nucleus remains intact, although it was pulled out of its original central position by the small galaxy over millions of years and, in fact, started to follow its visitor into intergalactic space. Some ring galaxies are not so lucky and lose their hearts forever.

Black Holes in Virgo

The larger the field of space and time astronomers observe, the better chance they have of discovering rare (from the human time scale) cosmic events such as supernovae and black holes. The famous Virgo cluster of more than 2,500 galaxies, which spans over 5 million light-years and contains upward of 125 trillion stars, probably gives birth to several black holes each year. These will probably be discovered during the 1990s with the Hubble Space Telescope and other sophisticated in-orbit telescopes, especially those that will detect the X-ray part of the spectrum.

If an average of five black holes are discovered every year for the next century, by A.D. 2087 there will be a catalogue of black holes with at least 500 entries—quite some progress from today's few "probables."

A Warped Couple

Some spiral galaxies have bizarre shapes. Spiral NGC 3817, some 40 million light-years away from the Sun, looks as if it were an old, warped phonograph record. And what a warp! The central portion of the spiral's disk is oriented almost 90 degrees—fully sideways—from the outer portions of the spiral arms.

What could have caused such a cosmic freak? Astronomers have been observing this odd galaxy, situated in the

The Virgo cluster of galaxies has at least 2,500 galaxies and upward of 125,000 billion stars. Every year, several black holes form in this immense area of space, and they are waiting to be discovered. *Courtesy National Optical Astronomy Observatories; Cerro Tololo Inter-American Observatory.*

constellation Ursa Major, with the 1.8-mile (3,000-meter)-long array of fourteen large, steerable dish antennas of the radio telescope at Westebok, the Netherlands. The galaxy is very close to a companion galaxy, perhaps as close as 130,000 light-years. There may even be a bridge of matter between the two systems. It is possible that the interaction of this cosmic couple has sent NGC 3817 spinning on its side like a top gone wild.

A Three-Ring Circus

Appropriately enough, in the spring constellation of Leo, the Lion, astronomers have found a three-ring circus. In the center of Leo, right in the belly of the lion, are three bright telescopic galaxies: M95 (NGC 3351), M96 (NGC 3368), and M105 (NGC 3379). All three are members of the Leo Cluster of galaxies. Cornell University astronomers, using the 1,000-foot (305-meter) radio telescope at Arecibo, Puerto Rico, discovered a huge circular ring of hydrogen gas around M105 and one of its smaller neighbors, NGC 3384. The ringlike feature had never been detected by optical telescopes. Only this huge and powerful radio telescope could find it at radio wavelengths.

The feature has a diameter of 600,000 light-years if its distance of 30 million light-years (the same as the galaxies) is correct. If this cloud were centered on the Milky Way, it would completely encircle not just our galaxy but eleven of its local galactic companions, including the Large and Small Magellanic Clouds.

The ring may be a galaxy that never formed; its density is believed to be less than a hundred times that of the interstellar material in the Milky Way Galaxy. It is possible that it may not have had the mass necessary to form a galaxy, although one of the astronomers involved estimates that it is roughly the size of a large galaxy.

Since this ring/cloud's discovery, other astronomers have tried to photograph it, but they have had no success. Some think it may be a galaxy with a very low surface brightness. Whatever it is, its one large feature and three smaller clouds appear to form the outline of an immense ring with a rotation period of about 4 billion years. A cosmic three-ring circus, complete with Lion!

Blowing Smoke Rings

When the radio data from observations of powerful radio galaxies are plotted, the resulting images depict huge lobes of matter on either side of a central object. Astronomers using the Very Large Array system of radio telescopes at Socorro, New Mexico, in 1984 reported observing what appeared to be rings of material ejected from the bright and powerful radio galaxy Hercules A. According to the researchers, each of the rings observed was larger than our Milky Way Galaxy. How were these huge cosmic structures formed? They were probably created by the central object, which is somehow pumping this great mass of material into space. This radio galaxy is blowing radio smoke rings.

Ring Around the Pole Galaxies

Astronomers looking closely at the photographic plates of the millions of external galaxies find rings aplenty. Some elliptical galaxies look curiously like the planet Saturn: a bright central object with a clear ring of materials around it at some distance. Other galaxies, apparently spirals, look like tigers jumping through hoops. Around the rotating disk of the galaxy is a distinct, separate ring. Some are extended like the rings of planets; others are very close to the central disk, but at right angles to it. These rings are probably composed of dust and young stars. But what forces cause such distorted and wildly shaped galaxies?

Astronomers from the Carnegie Institution in Washington, D.C., recently found such an object using the 4-meter (158-inch) telescope at the Cerro Tololo Inter-American Observatory, in Chile. The weird galaxy, designated A 0136-0801, is a dim object in the constellation of Cetus, the Whale. After spectrographic studies of the galaxy were completed, the data were thoroughly studied. The inner disk appeared to be that of a normal type SO galaxy—a configuration about midway between an elliptical and a spiral. Data suggest it is rotating around one axis the way a normal spiral would. The ring of dust at right angles to the main disk was probably formed when another galaxy passed close to the ring object. But why are the rings seen only at right angles in the almost two dozen examples found by these researchers? When a ring is formed at a lower angle, astronomers believe, it is basically unstable and soon breaks up. The right-angle rings, on the other hand, appear stable.

Study of the rings also demonstrates the presence of a great deal of matter outside the lighted galaxy disk. Gradually, according to theorists, the inner edge of the orbiting ring will be dissolved by the galaxy's main disk. But don't hold your breath waiting for the galaxy to do its through-the-hoop trick. The outer ring of galaxy A 0136-0801 may last another 23 billion years.

A Hot Matter

During much of 1983, NASA's Infrared Astronomy Satellite (IRAS), with its 22.4-inch (57-centimeter) infrared telescope, surveyed the sky. Infrared wavelengths are extremely difficult to detect on Earth because of the atmosphere. Some observations are possible from telescopes situated high on mountaintops that have very dry environments, but the best infrared observations are done in orbit with instruments such as IRAS.

The technical problems are formidable. To eliminate interference from the heat of the instrument and associated hardware, the entire IRAS telescope had to be cooled by superfluid helium to a temperature of only 2.5 degrees above absolute zero (-270.5 degrees Celsius, -454.9 degrees

Fahrenheit). The results of this technological achievement were astounding, and the data streams will be studied for decades to come.

One of the many surprises was the discovery of a galaxy, Arp 220, which is sending out 99 percent of its energy as heat. About 300 million light-years away, Arp 220 was discovered in 1966. Without the sophisticated infrared instruments of the 1980s, it was found by the evidence of only 1 percent of its energy. It is one of the most luminous infrared galaxies ever discovered—a hundred times more energetic in this wavelength range than our own Milky Way Galaxy.

Why so much galactic heat from Arp 220? One explanation put forth by astronomers is that this hot object results from a collision between two galaxies. Such a collision could compress their dust and gas clouds, initiating the formation of many new, hot, young stars. This burst of star formation could heat up the galaxies' dark outer halos of dust and gas. Instead of forming a few new stars a year, as does our galaxy, Arp 220 may have hundreds of star birthdays every year.

Celestial Boom Boxes

A laser is a unified, coherent beam of light at a very narrow frequency. A maser is the same thing, but in the radio portion of the electromagnetic spectrum. Astronomers have found greatly amplified radio sources coming from many objects in our Milky Way Galaxy: comets, regions of star formation, various types of stars. Now they have found intense sources of maser energy in distant galaxies. By mid-1985 four extragalactic objects had been identified that fit the description: Arp 220, Arp 299 (also known as NGC 3690 or IC 694), Markarian 232, and Markarian 273. The energetic galaxy Arp 220 beams its radio energy at the frequency of 1,667 megahertz at a strength seven hundred times that of the entire energy output of the Sun. All the galaxies found to produce maser emissions have either very energetic cores or are so-called starburst galaxies, with bursts of new star formation occurring.

Astronomer Willem Baan, of the Arecibo Radio Telescope, in Puerto Rico, believes he has the answer to this unusual celestial energy source. He claims that the maser energy is stimulated by radio waves from the center of the galaxies when they pass through clouds of gas in our line of sight. Each collision of a photon of radio energy with a cloud particle, he thinks, can cause two radio signals to be emitted instead of only one. Such powerful amplification of radio energy results in its detection at enormous distances of several hundred million light-years. Celestial boom boxes are really out there!

Galactic Digestion

The most interesting celestial object in the small southern constellation of Fornax (the Oven) is the radio galaxy NGC 1316 (Fornax A), which lies some 100 million light-years away from Earth. This galaxy has a misshapen and rippled

Fornax A, a peculiar radio galaxy over 100 million light-years from Earth, is believed to be cannibalizing a smaller galaxy within its central regions that its gravity captured. A huge cloud of hydrogen, its mass equal to 100 million Suns, is being absorbed there—a case of galactic indigestion. *Courtesy Edward B. Fomalont, National Radio Astronomy Observatory.*

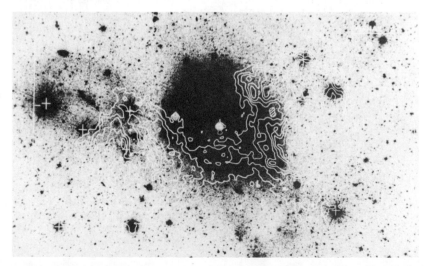

aspect, but this is not caused by the tidal stresses of any nearby galaxy. Inside NGC 1316 there is a huge rotating cloud of hydrogen, and some astronomers believe that it is really the remains of a small galaxy (or two), with a mass of about 100 million Suns, that has been captured and is being cannibalized by NGC 1316. If this is true, the central commotion and active radio bursts from this galaxy's nucleus are the sounds of galactic indigestion as one galaxy consumes another.

The Dusty Equator of Centaurus A

Centaurus A received the first letter of the alphabet from radio astronomers because it is the most intense radio source in that southern constellation. Optical astronomers gave a peculiar galaxy the number 5128 in the New General Catalogue. In the 1950s, they proved to be the same object.

A giant elliptical-galactic system, Centaurus A is about 15 million light-years away, which makes it the nearest of the giant radio sources. It emits a thousand times more radiation than a so-called normal galaxy such as our own Milky Way. Optically it is unusual, because there are vast dark dust lanes cutting across the great elliptical body, and this is rare for galaxies other than the disk-shaped spiral types. This equator of dust and gas varies in width from 4,000 to 8,000 light-years and is believed to completely encircle the galaxy; it is from this region that the strongest radio emissions emanate.

Two huge radio lobes, invisible to optical astronomers, lie at the galaxy's poles and have a combined dimension of about 3 million light-years—substantially larger than the distance between the Milky Way and Andromeda galaxies. They are believed to result from a violent explosion that took place some millions of years ago; this view is supported by a large number of hot young stars in the dust equator and near the galactic center—another rarity among elliptical galaxies.

The centers of active galaxies are what hold the key to their immense energies and violence, but the dust equator of

Peculiar Centaurus A, a powerful radio galaxy with a dust-filled equator, emits a thousand times more radiation than a "normal" galaxy such as our own. Some 15 million light-years away, it is the nearest of the giant radio sources and therefore one of the closest high-energy galaxies to us in the Universe. A Palomar Observatory Photograph. *Courtesy California Institute of Technology.*

NGC 5128 obscures this from our view. Here we have one of the closest high-energy galaxies to us in the Universe, one that would help astronomers unravel the mysteries of the distant quasars and Seyfert galaxies (see Chapter 4, "Quasars and Company"), but it is cloaked in dust.

Nevertheless, the young stars discovered in 5128's central region and murky equator help to date this galaxy's cosmic detonation to about 30 million years ago—just a few moments ago on the cosmic time scale. If this date is accurate, then the exploding star debris flew out at 33.5 million miles (54 million kilometers) per hour—a speed that could propel a spaceship from Earth to Mars in just over four hours, or just an hour longer than what is now a good New York-to-Paris air-travel time in the Concorde.

A Galaxy's Offspring

Galaxy NGC 5291, in Centaurus, about 270 million light-years away, contains the largest mass of neutral hydrogen ever discovered in the Universe—an estimated mass of 100 billion Suns. As this galaxy falls toward the center of a cluster of galaxies, the hot hydrogen gas that is distributed between all the galaxies of the cluster interacts with the neutral hydrogen gas of NGC 5291 and strips it away. This gas is thus swept out and leaves a trail of great gaseous knots in which stars are born. These gaseous knots are as large as our Milky Way's satellite galaxies, the Magellanic Clouds, and so NGC 5291's passage through the hot hydrogen in the cluster of galaxies in effect gives birth to new small galaxies—a string of offspring filled with millions of stars.

Plenty's the Matter

The supergalaxy M87, in the Virgo cluster of galaxies, has enough matter in it to create over twenty galaxies as large as ours. Its diameter is 848,000 light-years, about 8 1/2 times the diameter of our home galaxy. If we represented our solar system by the size of a saucer, this supergalaxy would be larger than the entire Earth.

The Loud Voice from Virgo

Besides being a giant, with a mass equal to about 3 trillion Suns, supergalaxy M87 is also a powerful radio source known as Virgo A (also 3C 274), the loudest cosmic voice in that constellation, and ranked the fifth-most-intense radio source in the sky—the first two being the Sun and Jupiter—even at a distance of some 50 million light-years.

The great energy flowing from Virgo A comes from its famous jet, composed of six tremendous visible clouds of extremely hot gas about 6,000 light-years long that were ejected by a cataclysmic explosion in the past. The reason the central regions of this supergalaxy do not display the stellar

The elliptical supergalaxy M87, also known as radio source Virgo A, has enough matter to equal twenty of our Milky Way Galaxies. Swarming around it are at least five hundred globular clusters, many of which have over 1 million stars. If our Solar System were the size of a saucer, this supergalaxy would be larger than the entire Earth! *Courtesy National Optical Astronomy Observatories; Cerro Tololo Inter-American Observatory.*

devastation of the blast that other explosive galaxies do is because there was practically no gas that the force could use as a galactic battering ram. The main explosive jet, and two other, minor ones, are therefore seen quite clearly, without the common problem of galactic smog caused by intervening gas and dust.

Recent research strongly indicates that the main jet goes directly into the galactic core, a core containing a massive object that some astronomers think is a black hole equal to the mass of 5 billion Suns. Whatever is at the core of supergalaxy M87, its energy is astounding. Its X-ray energy alone is about equal to that of 2.5 billion Suns. So, between the radio and the X-ray voices, Virgo A has no problem being heard, just being understood.

The Galaxy Counters

Two astronomers at Lick Observatory, Donald Shane and Carl Wirtanen, counted more than 1 million galaxies in a twelve-year period. They did this not with a telescope, as might be expected, but with a microscope that magnified 1,300 sky photographs. The 1-million-galaxy total amounts to tallying on the average 84,000 galaxies a year, 7,000 a month, and 233 each day. Since the average galaxy has about 50 billion stars, this means that these two astronomers confirmed the existence of 11,600 billion stars each day for twelve years. Shane and Wirtanen were obviously not counting sheep when they went to sleep.

Isolated Islands

All the galaxies—the spirals, the ellipticals, the irregulars and peculiars—fill only one one-hundred-millionth of the space in the known Universe. If they were evenly distributed, rather than clustered together, they would be as isolated as one person standing alone in a football stadium.

The Oldest Galaxy

The most distant and therefore oldest galaxy yet discovered was found in mid-1985. University of California researchers using the huge, 120-inch (3-meter) telescope at the Lick Observatory pointed their instrument toward a bright quasar, hoping to observe and record distant galaxies in a cluster they suspected to be nearby the quasar.

The team observed a galaxy they believe is associated with the quasar, and the age of both objects is estimated at an amazing 14.5 billion years, with the distance the same as the age—14.5 billion light-years away. Current estimates for the age of the Universe range from 15 billion years to 18 billion years. The previous record-holding distance for the farthest galaxy was estimated to be about 12.2 billion light-years away. The newly found record-holding galaxy's light would be almost three times as old as our Sun and solar system. This is not just prehistoric starlight; this is presolar starlight—light that began its journey long before our Sun and planets existed.

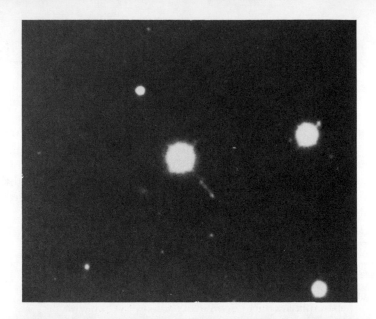

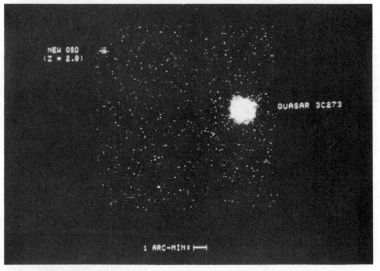

Two views, optical and X-ray, of the famous quasar 3C 273. This quasar gives off more energy than 5 trillion Suns. It is so bright that, if our Sun were represented by a candle, 3C 273 would shine brighter than all the lights in New York City put together. If it were where Alpha Centauri is, the nearest star to our Sun, it would shine as bright as 68 Suns! *Courtesy National Optical Astronomy Observatories; and Smithsonian Institute.*

CHAPTER 4

QUASARS AND COMPANY

If there had been humans on the Earth 12 billion years ago—if there had been an Earth!—they would have seen quasars burning on every side in the sky with the intensity of our brightest stars.

—Chet Raymo, *The Soul of the Night*

Before Quasars

The word *quasar* did not exist before 1964. These mysterious cosmic objects were named a year after astronomers discovered that these pinpoints of ancient light were much more than what they first appeared: radio sources detected by the radio telescopes of the day. Before 1963, a few of them were recorded in the Third Cambridge Catalogue of Radio Stars as compact radio sources. Some astronomers called them radio stars. No one foresaw their importance to astronomy and humankind's growing knowledge of the Universe. No one knew then that these cosmic objects, never to be directly viewed by the naked human eye, would spark a scientific debate that would last for decades.

All that changed in 1963, when astronomer Maarten Schmidt, of Mount Wilson and Palomar Observatories, located the visual component of radio source 3C 273 with the 200-inch (5.1-meter) telescope and found it to have two optical components: a round, starlike body and a dimmer tail of light projecting outward from it. Once the visual light of the radio source was obtained, spectroscopy was used to obtain the object's spectrum. But at first no one could identify the strange spectral lines of 3C 273. Schmidt continued to study its spectrum. Some of the lines were oddly familiar. Didn't four of the lines resemble lines of hydrogen? But, Schmidt realized, they did not belong where they were found. Then the astronomer had his breakthrough recognition: they were hydrogen lines, but they had been displaced toward the red end of the spectrum. The object 3C 273 had a huge red shift, which indicated it was moving away from the Solar System at a velocity of over 25,000 miles (40,200 kilometers) a second. This tremendous velocity also meant that the object was nearly 3 billion light-years away.

Was this really possible? Schmidt and his colleagues studied the spectra of other radio sources whose visual components were identified. Their spectral lines could also be identified if huge red shifts implying great recession velocities were assumed. The astronomers were seeing the most distant celestial objects ever discovered in the Universe. And if the red shifts were valid, as well as the high velocities and great distances that logically followed, then even more mysteries unfolded. These were not just the most distant and fastest-receding cosmic objects ever found, they were also the most powerful—too powerful for their size to be explained by the astrophysicists. What was going on out there, in the distant and early Universe? These quasi-stellar radio sources were far different from any stars known. The only similarity they had with stars was that, even in the largest telescopes, they appeared only as dim points of light. What were they? Astronomers had a new cosmic riddle to solve, and they realized that these distant beacons of superpowerful energy that lit up the early Universe might lead to other ultimate answers about the cosmos, its origins, and its fate. The quasars promised to be the new guiding lights for the ever-curious minds that probed the boundaries of the Universe.

A year after the mysteries of these enigmatic objects

came forth from the study of their ancient light, the word *quasar* was born. It was a Chinese-American physicist by the name of Hong Yee Chiu who abbreviated the compound adjective, *quasi-stellar* to *quasar.* Even scientists appreciate the fact that one word is often better than two or more. (And so do the manufacturers who produce TV sets and other products who decided to borrow the name to help them penetrate their markets. What was still a challenging mystery to the astronomers became household product names.)

The Quasar Connection

Quasars remain the lead characters in the cosmic mystery plot, even after almost three decades. They still look like stars, even through the world's largest and most powerful telescopes. They still emit energy in the radio, infrared, ultraviolet, and X-ray portions of the spectrum. They still vary in light and radio energy. They still have large red shifts in their spectra, which means to all but a few holdout astronomers that they are the most distant objects discovered so far in the Universe, as well as the fastest objects, receding from us at over 90 percent the speed of light. We can still identify quasars—and new ones are being discovered with better equipment each year—but we do not know for sure how they fit into the overall evolution of the Universe or how they produce their prodigious energy.

A pattern of evidence is emerging, however, and some answers are coming not just from the quasars themselves and the objects near to them in distant space and time, but from quasars in the context of all their strange relatives: BL Lacertae, N-galaxies, radio galaxies, Seyfert galaxies, and the so-called normal galaxies (like our Milky Way). It is through understanding these eccentric relatives of the quasars that the full meaning of the quasar's character and place in the Universe will be understood. This extended quasar family, which includes the various types of galaxies with active nuclei, has one thing in common: a violent family history.

The Quasar with Big Ears

Many quasars are discovered by radio astronomers first, and then the radio coordinates are used to locate the optical object, which looks like millions of ordinary dim stars. After detailed study of its spectrum, the object is confirmed as either a quasar or another kind of radio object. This is how the first quasars were found, but now it is known that quasars can be either radio-loud or radio-silent.

Quasar 3C 47, one of the first-known radio-loud quasars, has a radio image of two lobes, which appear like a rough figure eight. This double structure is similar to radio galaxies that share certain characteristics and may be close cousins. These lobes lie on either side of the optical quasar—big radio ears attached to a tiny head of light.

Quasar 3C 47 was one of the largest observed cosmic objects for more than a decade. Its dimension includes not just the optical source, which is only one small portion of the powerful electromagnetic radiation pouring forth, but the radio object as well, as measured between the centers of the two radio ears. This distance is almost 1 million light-years, ten times the diameter of our galaxy—enough space to comfortably accommodate more than 1 trillion stars.

Quasar 3C 47 is about 4.5 billion light-years away, so the light that astronomers see today left just about when the Sun and the planets, including Earth, were forming from the protosun—the contracting cloud of dust and gas.

A Quasar Biggie

Quasar 3C 345's giant radio image, first detected in 1980, is one of the largest known objects in the Universe. The two extended radio lobes span about 78 million light-years—that's enough space to accommodate 780 galaxies the size of the Milky Way with all their 80-trillion-odd stars. The time that it would take light to travel from one end of this object to the other is as long as it took the land masses of Africa and South America to drift 2,000 miles (3,200 kilometers) apart in recent Earth history.

The Quiet and the Loud Quasars

The first few quasars discovered in the early 1960s were strong radio sources—in fact, that is how they were detected —and then the quiet (or weak) radio quasars were discovered a few years later, once astronomers were armed with the spectral and other clues for their quasar hunt among millions of look-alike stars.

Today the quiet quasars are unquestionably the silent majority. About 99 percent of those discovered are quiet, while only 1 percent are in the boisterous minority whose radio signals blast out and eventually reach Earth. The silent quasars are believed to lack a thick corona of high-energy particles. This low-density corona, in fact, is the reason that quasars in the noisy minority emit strong radio signals. Quasar members of both camps can vary their radio and visible power up to twenty times. If strong quasar radio noise were piped through your home radio and suddenly increased twenty times from a low volume, it would blast you right out of your chair—hardly music of the celestial spheres.

The Mirror Quasar

Two blue quasar objects discovered in 1979, 0957+561 A and B, were found to have close to identical spectra and red shifts. The discovery puzzled astronomers. How could two separate quasars, receding at the same velocity and situated at the same distance, be so nearly identical, considering the fact that most quasars have quite different spectra? The likely explanation is that there is really only one quasar and that extreme gravity from a massive object, perhaps a galaxy, that lies between the quasar and Earth is creating a gravita-

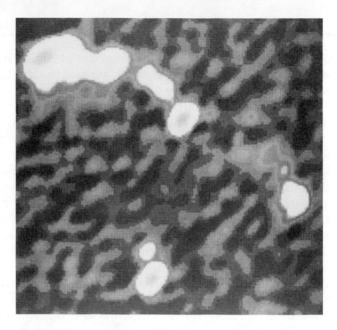

The mirror quasar 0957+561 A and B seen in a radio image. The two similar-looking, roughly circular objects in this field are believed to be two images of the same object, created by the gravitational-lens effect of an intervening galaxy that bends the light and radio radiation. *Courtesy National Radio Astronomy Observatory.*

tional lens effect (Einstein's General Theory of Relativity) and producing two images of the same quasar—one of the few mirror quasars discovered so far!

At the Heart of a Quasar

Even though quasars are compact, their optical images usually not much more than 1 light-year across, they emit more energy than 100 supergiant galaxies. This stupendous energy creation from such relatively small celestial objects has baffled astrophysicists ever since quasars were discovered, in the 1960s. At first this paradox seemed irreconcilable. Some scientists began to question whether the immense estimated distances were wrong and proposed ways of interpreting them as relatively close objects. Today, however, this is a minority view, and quasars are generally believed to be the most distant and oldest objects in the Universe. The big question, however, remains: How can such small objects produce such tremendous energy? How can quasars, some of which are not much larger than our solar system, produce energies tens of times more powerful than entire galaxies such as our Milky Way?

There have been theories galore to explain this ultimate energy source: matter-antimatter annihilation, collisions of massive stars, supernova explosions (when a star at least eight times the mass of the Sun blows up), magnetic-field conversion of gravitational energy into particle energy, rotational energy of an extremely compact mass, and gravitational collapse of supermassive stars, are some of them.

Today many astronomers favor the idea that massive black holes lurk in the nuclei of quasars, where intense gravity attracts and gobbles up stars and hot gas. This model explains the intense X-ray emission from quasars, which would be created when gas and matter are heated to high temperatures as they first accrete around and then fall into the black hole. The massive black hole theory implies that quasars are small cores of violently exploding galaxies and that perhaps all large galaxies—even the Milky Way—go through similar short violent phases during their lifetimes. Evidence for this interpretation—that quasars could be highly energetic newborn galaxies with massive black holes in their nuclei—is growing.

Such a giant black hole would have a mass of 10 billion Suns—one tenth that of our entire galaxy. This gargantuan gravity hole at the heart of a quasar would be about six times larger than our solar system. If a future starship ever crossed its gravitational boundary (its event horizon), it could never escape, not even if it could accelerate to the speed of light.

A Spark in the Fuzz

The mysterious quasar fog is lifting as the twentieth century draws to a close. More sensitive instruments are peering into the distant light-years and finding additional evidence that quasars were the violent centers of newborn or young galaxies in the earlier Universe. More "fuzz" was detected around some galaxies; the fuzz represented the unresolved distant light from billions of stars in a galaxy that surrounded a quasar. Only in the past few years has this galactic evidence supported the theory that quasars are situated in familiar celestial territory—at the center of the most common large structures in the Universe: galaxies.

During 1983, astronomers conducted a research program from the observatory atop Mauna Kea, in Hawaii, that collected data on the color and brightness profiles of the so-called fuzz surrounding the quasars. As the astronomers studied the quasar QSO 1059+730 in May of that year, they noticed something unusual on the photographic plates. A bright object was seen on the image near to the quasar that was not visible in earlier photographs. What was it? A supernova—the first to ever be associated with a distant quasar whose light is reaching Earth after a journey of almost 1 billion years. But supernovae are not isolated cosmic events; they involve large stars that are undergoing their death throes, and stars are found only in galaxies. This is more observational evidence that quasars were at the centers of galaxies billions of years ago.

Quasar Companions

Astronomers are intensely studying the cosmic areas around quasars to find companion galaxies that can be used to confirm the distances and red shifts of these beacons of the early Universe. In recent years the observational limits have been stretched with new high-tech imaging equipment that uses CCD (charge-coupled devices) that are capable of collecting every last photon of radiation possible. A CCD camera is a very sensitive solid-state electronic device that is backed up by computer processing. It is capable of producing an image in just a few minutes.

CCDs used with the telescope at Kitt Peak National Observatory, in Arizona, have given astronomers the additional observational edge needed to help resolve the quasar mystery. A University of Maryland team used this equipment to search for quasars that were close to galaxies in the distant Universe. They limited the space between the objects to two galactic diameters and brought to bear several advanced spectrographic techniques to be certain the companion galaxy was not a foreground object that only appeared to be a quasar companion. The red shifts of nineteen nebulous objects that were believed to be companion galaxies to the quasars were measured. The distances and recession velocities derived from the red-shift measurements were then compared to quasar measurements, and in eighteen out of the nineteen cases, the measurements were very close, strongly suggesting that the objects and the quasars were traveling together in space and time at the same velocity, which is what Big Bang cosmology predicts. Spectral studies completed with the sensitive CCDs also indicated that the companions were galaxies, and spectral studies of the fuzz around quasars showed that such dim, unresolved light is produced by billions of stars.

What does all this mean? That quasars are found in the company of galaxies, indeed at centers of galaxies that travel with galactic companions. In other words, quasars are not loners at the edge of the observable Universe. They are found in regions of space and time that have a high number of galaxies, a galactic density even higher than the normal clustering of galaxies that takes place.

One CCD image taken of the sky near quasar PKS 2300-189 shows that this quasar and a companion galaxy are both immersed in a faint and fuzzy envelope of starlight. This could mean that the companion galaxy and the galaxy in which the quasar is centered are undergoing some sort of gravitational battle that creates tidal distortions on a cosmic scale.

This new research on the interrelationship between quasars and galaxies is actively continuing; and as it does, the distinctions between these two celestial objects are slowly disappearing. If many astronomers today can say with conviction that quasars are the violent centers of some galaxies in the earlier Universe, by the end of the century they may know if all galaxies or only certain types had great and powerful quasars at their hearts. They may also understand how the quasars were created in the first place a few billion years after the Big Bang, which began the Universe.

Counting Quasars

Quasars are clues to the early evolution of the Universe and are the only optical evidence astronomers have from the first few billion years after the Big Bang. The farthest-away quasars allow scientists to look back in time and observe the oldest celestial objects, which may have evolved first into radio galaxies and then into the various types of galaxies present during more recent eras of the Universe. More than three thousand quasars have been observed and verified with specialized spectroscopic techniques since they were first discovered, in the early 1960s.

While quasar counting may seem to be one of the most esoteric and impractical endeavors imaginable, it can tell what kind of Universe we inhabit. By counting quasars at certain distances (and times), the densities of the Universe over billions of years can be compared. The complex tally is further proof—along with the cosmic background radiation and helium abundance—that the Universe is still expanding from the cataclysmic Big Bang. This is so because astronomers see an increasing number of quasars as they look back in time through the light-years to an earlier Universe—at least up to a point on the cosmic clock. About 5 billion years ago, when the Earth, the Sun, and the rest of the Solar System were forming, there were about a hundred times more quasars than there are today. Estimates put the total number of quasars in the observable (past) Universe at about 15 million, but most of these, over 99 percent, no longer exist, because they have burned themselves out during the billions of years it has taken their light to reach the Earth. But there is only one sure way astronomers have to prove this: wait for billions of years to see if the quasar light slowly dims over time.

Quasar Power

Quasars are so powerful that many of them emit about a hundred times as much visible radiation as a normal spiral galaxy like the Milky Way, even though they are often 5.2 million times smaller (100,000 light-years for a galaxy, compared to as little as 1 light-week for a quasar). This is similar to a powerful laser beam, only 1 inch (2.54 centimeters) across, which is brighter than the total light from a forest fire that burns an area 80 miles (129 kilometers) across. The quasar, however, unlike the laser beam, sends its incredible energy in all directions.

The Violently Variable Quasar

Light and radio emissions vary over time for most quasars—about 80 percent of them—and most of these brighten and fade over periods of months and years. Among these variable quasars are a few optically violent ones such as quasar 3C 446, which once increased its brightness twenty-fold in just a few days with a tremendous burst of energy. This means that its size cannot be more than a few light-days across (2 light-days equals about 32 billion miles, or 51 billion kilometers), or nine times the mean distance from the Sun to the planet Pluto. The fact that a celestial object so relatively small can produce such prodigious amounts of energy is still a mystery to astrophysicists. If our Sun were to increase its brightness by twenty times in a few days, each day that dawned would be about 38 degrees Celsius (100 degrees Fahrenheit) hotter than the one before, until worldwide temperatures reached about 260 degrees Celsius (500 degrees Fahrenheit). The oceans would boil and the Earth would become enshrouded in a perpetual cloud of steam, with a pressure as high as a steam boiler—three hundred times that of our present atmosphere.

Brighter than
Five Trillion Suns

No quasar can be seen by the naked eye, but the brightest quasar known for almost three decades, 3C 273 (number 273 in the third Cambridge Catalogue of Radio Sources), in the constellation Virgo, the first to be identified as a distant object, becomes visible with the aid of a relatively small backyard telescope. Quasar 3C 273 is about 3 billion light-years away, so its light observed from Earth today left when there was only bacterial life existing on our planet. This object is receding from us at a velocity of about one sixth the speed of light, or about 100 million miles (161 million kilometers) per hour. A jet of material extends 250,000 light-years out from the main body of the quasar like a tail, no doubt ejected from some huge explosion in its past. But quasar 3C 273's most impressive feature is its brightness—a record-holder for twenty years, brighter than anything else ever observed in the Universe: 5 trillion times as luminous as the Sun. If quasar 3C 273 were situated where Alpha Centauri, the nearest star to the Sun, is (at a distance of 4.3 light-years), it would shine as bright as 68 Suns, and its radio emission would be so intense that it would be possible to draw sparks from metal just by passing a metal rod nearby.

View from a Quasar

If the world's largest telescope could be placed as far away as quasar 3C 273, almost 3 billion light-years, our great spiral galaxy, the Milky Way, with its more than 200 billion stars and unknown numbers of planets and life-forms, could barely be resolved as a disk, and its spiral arms could not be observed. Compared to the blazing quasars and other near objects, it would not be of much interest.

A Quasar's Invisible Energy

Most of the energy produced by quasar 3C 273 (at least 90 percent of it) is invisible infrared radiation, which lies between the radio and the visible bands of the electromagnetic spectrum. This famous quasar emits 100,000 times more energy in infrared radiation than our entire galaxy emits from light radiation. If 3C 273 were as far away as Polaris, the North Star (780 light-years), we would still receive enough infrared radiation to warm the Earth significantly. If it were even closer, about 500 light-years away, we would receive as much infrared energy from it as we receive light energy from the Sun.

The Universal Divide

Quasar 3C 273, the first discovered, is also one of the closest. It is a cosmic beacon marking a kind of universal divide in space and time. Its light is almost 3 billion years old when our telescope and eyes view it, placing it farther away in space and time than most "normal" galaxies or other familiar cosmic objects. Beyond it lie active galaxies and most quasars; that is all—until we reach the observable "edge" of the young Universe, as it was some 18 billion years ago.

The Short-Lived Quasars

A middle-sized quasar is brighter than 300 billion Suns, but it must pay the price of its blazing glory with a short lifetime of about 1 million years—ten thousand times shorter than the Sun's expected lifetime.

The Brightest of Them All?

A radio source discovered in 1981 in the constellation Cepheus, in the northern hemisphere, may be the brightest quasar yet discovered. Astronomers in England and the United States identified it with an optical object and calculated that it has an intrinsic magnitude of about −33, which makes it the most luminous object found in the Universe. This brightest of cosmic objects, however, can be seen only with the largest telescopes, because its apparent visual magnitude is +16.5—thousands of times dimmer than the dimmest star that can be seen by the human eye.

The Far Quasars

One of the most distant objects in the Universe, quasar Q 172, was discovered by Lick Observatory astronomers in 1973. It is over 12 billion light-years away from Earth, so the astronomers see it as it was more than 12 billion years ago. This quasar is receding from the solar system at a rate of 603 million miles (900 million kilometers) per hour—90 percent of the speed of light.

Other quasars, farther away, were discovered in the late 1970s and 1980s; they now hold the record distances of space and time. Quasar Q 1442+101 edged into first place and held the record for about a year, and then an even more distant quasar was found in 1982 by radio astronomers at the Parkes Radio Astronomy Observatory, in New South Wales. Designated PKS 2000-330, the optical counterpart of the radio source was found by astronomers with the Siding Spring Observatory's large optical telescope. This quasar's red shift indicated that it was about 13 billion light-years away and flying outward at more than 91 percent the speed of light.

If this quasar radiates equally in all directions, its entire radiated power is about ten thousand times that radiated by our Milky Way Galaxy. Its distance is over 13 billion light-years, which also makes it the oldest optically observed object in the Universe (the 2.7-Kelvin cosmic background radiation is the oldest signal observed by radio).

Discoveries of distant quasars such as Q 1208+1011 in 1986 are becoming less frequent; there are not many of them. This fact has led astronomers to believe that these quasars may be at the observable edge of the Universe, perhaps within 1 or 2 billion years of the Big Bang. When their light began the journey through the Universe, the Earth, the Sun, and the rest of the Solar System did not exist.

The Closest Quasar?

While quasars are the most distant celestial objects in the Universe, some are closer than others. One of the nearest is 800 million light-years away—more than 1.8 billion times farther away than Proxima Centauri, the nearest star to the Sun. This object was discovered in 1978 by matching an X-ray source with its faint optical counterpart, which looked like just another star among millions; it was designated 2S 0241+61. If each of the 800 million light-years were reduced to equal 1 mile (1.6 kilometers)—a light-year actually equals about 5.9 trillion miles or 9.5 billion kilometers—it would still take a person 36,528 years to walk the distance to this close quasar. To take the scale up to reality, you would multiply the time it would take by 5.9 trillion.

Just a Second

The energy emitted by a quasar in just 1 second would supply the energy needs of the Earth for a period of 1 billion years. Since quasars are billions of years old as we look back in time at them, they are probably no longer in existence, so there is no way to tap these ancient cosmic objects. It is also possible that our Sun and Earth and other planets exist in a galaxy that once was a violent and awesomely powerful quasar.

Quasar Isolation

The cosmic gulfs between the quasars—averaging about 570 million light-years—are barely comprehensible, being some 5,700 times the diameter of our galaxy (at least 100,000 light-years) and 131 million times the distance to Alpha Centauri, the nearest star system to our Sun at 4.2 light-years.

The Giant Cosmic Radio

Radio galaxies are distant, high-energy, active galaxies whose radio output can be 1 million times more powerful than our galaxy's. There are two basic types: compact radio galaxies and extended radio galaxies. Galaxy M87 (Virgo A), a mere 50 million light-years away in the Virgo cluster of galaxies, is the second-closest strong radio source (after Centaurus A) and is an example of a compact radio galaxy. Its compressed core is only 2.5 light-months across, while its large halo, which emits most of the radiation, is almost 200,000 light-years across. One of the largest extended radio galaxies so far discovered is the double radio source 3C 236, with two tremendous clouds of high-speed electrons that span almost 20 million light-years—a diameter large enough to accommodate 200 galaxies the size of the Milky Way.

The Loudest Radio Galaxy

The most powerful radio galaxy in the sky is Cygnus A, which surrounds a faint optical galaxy with an unusual, double nucleus. The two enormous radio lobes, each one about 163,000 light-years to either side of the visible galaxy, are invisible to the world's largest telescopes, but they make up for it by being "heard" over a range of billions and billions of miles. Each of these radio lobes is about as large as our Milky Way Galaxy, and each pours forth energy equal to the luminosity of 1 trillion Suns. (Have you noticed lately how bright one Sun is?) Together they equal the light energy of 20 Milky Way galaxies and their 2 trillion or so stars. Cygnus A is

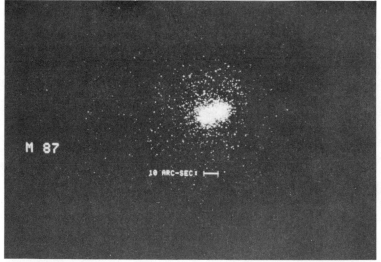

M 87

10 ARC-SEC

Virgo A, also known as supergiant galaxy M87, is a compact radio galaxy that gives off powerful radiation. Both its optical and X-ray images are shown here. It is the second-closest radio galaxy (after Centaurus A) to our Solar System. *Courtesy National Optical Astronomy Observatories; and Smithsonian Institution.*

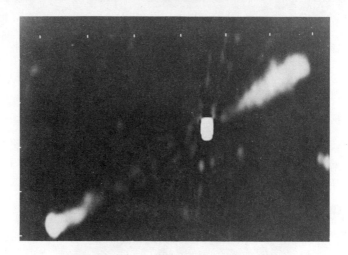

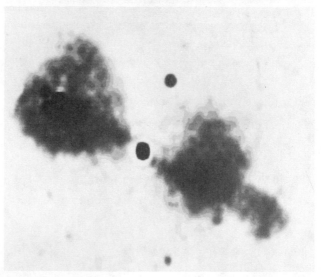

Two of the largest extended radio galaxies known, 3C 236 and DA 240. Astronomers have ranked 3C 236 as the largest object in the Universe; it could accommodate two hundred galaxies the size of the Milky Way, with some 20,000 billion stars. Westerbork Synthesis Radio Telescope, Netherlands Foundation for Radio Astronomy. *Courtesy R. G. Strom.*

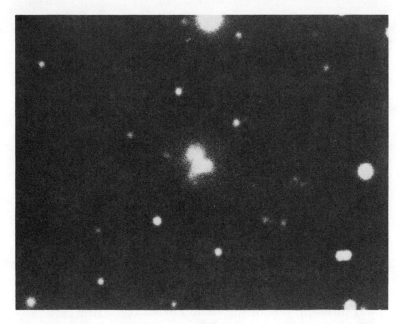

Cygnus A, the most powerful radio galaxy in the sky. This photograph shows only the optical component, not the immense radio
lobes that extend some 300,000 light-years on each side of the galaxy. These lobes could easily encompass several galaxies the size of
our Milky Way. A Palomar Observatory Photograph. *Courtesy California Institute of Technology.*

about 1 billion light-years away, farther than some of the
closer quasars which its double radio lobes sometimes resemble, and its radio and light energy seen today left this object
when worms and jellyfish were the most advanced forms of
life on Earth.

A Cosmic Sword

Radio galaxies and quasars have so much in common that
they may ultimately prove to be the same kind of cosmic
object. They both produce vast amounts of energy from a
still-mysterious source (perhaps a massive black hole), and it
is likely they both represent the earliest and most violent

stages in the evolution of galaxies in the Universe, while the other active galaxies represent later evolutionary stages (more theory, of course, than fact, as we approach the end of the twentieth century).

The double radio lobes common to most radio galaxies are also found in many of the radio-loud quasars. Since the radio galaxies with these lobes are always associated with giant elliptical galaxies, some astronomers believe that the quasars are also in giant elliptical galaxies—but their distance makes observational proof of this impossible.

Radio galaxy NGC 6251 has violently ejected a long jet of ultra-hot material from its galactic core. This jet is similar to the one emanating from quasar 3C 273, which extends 250,000 light-years out from the core. Similar, but not the same: the jet of radio galaxy NGC 6251 measures more than 750,000 light-years and extends from the galactic core to (and through) one of the radio lobes.

Images of Cosmic Commotion

The Very Large Array radio telescope near Socorro, New Mexico, has observed two distant objects that may be a new class of radio source. The source G 357.7-0.1, in the constellation Scorpius, resembles a tornado, while G 5.3-1.0, in Sagittarius, appears like a bird in flight. What they have in common is an extremely bright compact component at the western end of their masses, and the shapes of their luminous matter strongly suggest that these bright internal components have moved from east to west through these strange radio objects, leaving tails of matter behind. The radio hot spots come from the positions of the in-motion tornado and bird.

What is going on? Experts think that a fast-moving two-star system containing either a neutron star or a black hole that is accreting matter may be creating all the radio commotion and painting these cosmic images. They also predict that the objects will be found to have strong X-ray emissions when studied with X-ray observatories above Earth. This will indicate that the tornado and the bird are produced by high-energy particles similar to those found in SS 433, Vela X-1, and Hercules X-1.

Quasar Cousins

BL Lacertae objects (the first to be identified, in the constellation Lacerta, was incorrectly classified as a variable star) are close cousins to the quasars and share many characteristics. They are starlike in appearance even through the most powerful telescopes, and they are variable in brightness as well as in radio energy. The main difference between quasars and BL Lacs is that the BL Lacs contain no emission lines in their spectra, which means they do not have enveloping clouds of gas to produce such lines as do the quasars. Another difference is that BL Lacs are definitely superbrilliant and superpowerful nuclei of distant elliptical galaxies, while quasars are only suspected (although direct evidence is mounting) by some astronomers to be violent nuclei of the most distant and oldest galaxies.

In 1968, BL Lacertae was shown to be an optical counterpart of a peculiar radio source, and this class of bright objects was officially recognized. It was still later that they were proved to be the ultrabrilliant centers of elliptical galaxies.

A few dozen BL Lacs have been discovered, and measurements place them at the same distance as the closest quasars—about 1–2 billion light-years away. One BL Lac object, 1308+326, lies beyond some of the closest quasars. At the peak of an energy outburst in 1983, BL Lac 1308+326 was considered to be the most luminous object in the Universe. These superpowerful objects have been called the "naked quasars," because most of their light comes directly from the ultra-high-speed electrons emitted by the galactic cores, whereas vast clouds of hot gas are believed to often obscure spectral measurements of quasars.

BL Lacs, like so many quasars, flare up violently; they have been known to increase their brilliance by six hundred times. This may in part be caused by rapid rotation rates and extremely high magnetic fields which work against one another to create such powerful light.

Miniquasar

In the constellation Cancer, near the Praesepe star cluster, is the BL Lacertae object OJ 287, which pulses with its light on time scales of fifteen to thirty minutes. While astronomers do not consider it unusual for quasars and other brilliant extragalactic objects to randomly change their brightness from day to day or even over shorter periods of time, it *is* unusual for objects in the extended quasar family of hyperactive nuclei to vary in brightness with such regularity.

OJ 287 is the brightest and most inconstant BL Lacertae object known, and astronomers have had evidence of this for years. Some observers have even recorded variations of output over its full spectrum of electromagnetic radiation—from radio to infrared emission—in about fifty seconds. Such brightness fluctuations have been interpreted by many of the experts as proof that violent changes are taking place in a small nucleus.

Like so many other active cosmic objects in the distant Universe, the mysteries of this BL Lac's powerful central engine have not been solved. At least the experts can agree that a constant-beat signal means the object is rotating. But OJ 287 is dancing to several different beats, and so the fluctuations must be coming from several objects. The case has been made that hot spots in an accretion disk rotating around a massive black hole are responsible for the variations. If this is so, then the central black hole is estimated to have a mass from 3 to 60 million times the mass of our Sun.

The Shifting Cosmic Sands

N-galaxies (N stands for nucleus) are also called N-type galaxies. They are extremely active islands of stars with compact, powerful, and luminous nuclei. Discovered in 1958 by

W. W. Morgan, the first ones charted were optical counterparts to powerful and compact radio sources. Since then, like quasars, many radio-quiet N-galaxies have been found. In fact N-galaxies and quasars share so many characteristics—broad emission lines, variable brightness, size, tremendous energy output, to name just a few—that many astronomers believe quasars *are* N-galaxies so far away that only the bright and highly energetic nucleus—not the faint star envelope—is visible. The close similarities between the active N-galaxies and quasars are emphasized even more by the fact that astronomers have reclassified some early quasars as N-galaxies; 3C 48 is an example of a quasar reclassified as an N-galaxy, when long-exposure photographs detected a faint envelope (a distinguishing mark for an N-galaxy), which is really billions upon billions of stars in the galactic form surrounding the superbrilliant, superpowerful nucleus. Take away the faint starry envelope, and what have you got? A quasar—a less energetic quasar, perhaps, but still a quasar. When the nucleus of N-galaxy 3C 371 reaches its most brilliant phase in luminosity, canceling out its starry envelope, it looks just like a quasar. Such strong relationships among members of the hyperactive cosmic family are part of the increasing evidence that quasars are the violent centers of galaxies in the early Universe and that over the billions of years that the Universe has been expanding the quasars have calmed down from their early violent behavior to become many different kinds of galaxies—some more active than others—in the cosmic realm.

The Quasar Galaxy

The most quasarlike N-galaxy, 3C 120, has a superbrilliant nucleus over 16,000 light-years in diameter and an extended galactic region of over 130,000 light-years in diameter—only one third again as large as that of our Milky Way Galaxy. It has, like many quasars, doubled its brightness in a few months, and its central energy source (whatever it is!) has produced clouds of electrons once a year that expand and, like quasars, can be measured by radio astronomers. N-Galaxy 3C 120 is also one of the most powerful of all the active-nucleus galaxies and releases almost as much energy as a quasar—a trillion times more light energy than the Sun. If 3C 120's nucleus produced more light energy at a much greater distance, its starry galactic envelope would be invisible and—PRESTO!—it would become a quasar, and just maybe the major cosmic evolutionary link that modern astronomers have been patiently, and painstakingly, seeking.

The Galaxy Quasar

Quasar PHL 3070, examined by the 200-inch (508-centimeter) Palomar Mountain reflecting telescope, may be one of those important missing links between the distant quasars of the early Universe (remember: the farther away, the farther back in time) and the galaxies of today's Universe, or at least the recent Universe. What makes it a possible link? Just a little bit of fuzz that has been observed on its outer envelope. This faint fuzz may really be billions and billions of stars surrounding a galactic core. In fact, this quasar may be an N-galaxy. In astronomy, names change or are interchanged as our knowledge of the Universe expands like the cosmic reality being studied.

The Exploding Spirals

Seyfert galaxies, named after the astronomer who discovered them, in 1943, are members of the so-called extended quasar family of brilliant and powerful celestial bodies that all have violence in their cores: gigantic outpourings of explosive high energies. Seyferts are usually spiral in form, have compacted cores often less than 1 light-year across, and are usually blue, exceptionally brilliant, and variable in their light and other energy output. If you took a quasar's light and other energy and divided it into a hundred equal portions, one of those portions would equal the energy at the core of a Seyfert galaxy. Indeed, Seyfert galaxies, like N-galaxies, may be considered scaled-down quasars that are closer to us in space and time. Astronomers place Seyfert galaxies between the so-called normal galaxies like our Milky Way and Andromeda, whose nuclei are not particularly energetic, and the violently active quasars that probably represent the centers of newborn galaxies of the early Universe. Give Seyferts more energy and move them farther into the distant, earlier Universe, and they, too, become quasars. Seyfert galaxies are cosmic butterflies, and astronomy is currently putting its net over them to take a really detailed look.

The Seyfert-Quasar Connection

Is it possible that the centers of Seyfert galaxies are really just weak or dead quasars that have evolved over billions of years? Astronomers at the Palomar Observatory of the California Institute of Technology are studying the centers of "nearby," bright galaxies and obtaining their spectral qualities to see if they exhibit similarities to the full-fledged, violent centers of Seyfert galaxies that lie farther out in space and back in time—and closer to what many astronomers believe to be their ultimate sires, the quasars.

Results from the first seventy-five galaxies surveyed strongly indicate that this could be cosmic truth. The spectral data (emission lines at certain wavelengths) from this faint-end group of nuclei—which are within a larger category that astronomers refer to as active galactic nuclei (AGNs), which includes quasars and all other objects with energetic centers —suggests that there could be millions of these faded centers. Because there are no quasars present in the recent Universe (almost all those discovered have been billions of years old and the same distance away) and because the evidence continues to mount for the interpretation that quasars are situated in the nuclei of galaxies, the astronomers of this study believe that the galactic nuclei they studied were quasars in the distant past—which is to say, the young Universe. The astronomers hope to have a more definitive answer after surveying at least another five hundred galaxies whose centers are on the low-energy end of the galactic scale.

Seyfert Tidal Waves

A recent survey of Seyfert galaxies done at the University of Hawaii showed that almost a third of Seyfert galaxies (25–30 percent of them) have peculiar and distorted shapes. Many experts contend that this is evidence of tidal interactions with other galaxies—cosmic tugs of war between immense islands of stars—and that Seyferts are involved in such gravitational encounters much more often than other types of galaxies.

The Seyfert galaxy NGC 7674 has two immense tails of matter streaming out into intergalactic space; they appear to result from an extreme tidal interaction with another galaxy. If this scenario reflects reality, what causes the Seyferts to start gravitational wars with their neighboring galaxies?

One of the explanations for the great energies found at the centers of active galaxies like Seyferts is that they are powered by immense black holes. The Seyfert experts go on to speculate that the tidal interactions of the Seyferts may reflect the hungry black hole's method of obtaining huge amounts of gaseous fuel to drive its gravitational vortex.

Seyfert Power

Even though an average-sized Seyfert galaxy radiates as much energy as several million million suns, its energy-producing nucleus (core) is no more, perhaps less, than 10 million times the diameter of the Sun: about 8.6 trillion miles (13.8 trillion kilometers), 1.5 light-years, or 1.1 billion times the diameter of the Earth—which is all to say that Seyferts pack an awesome energy wallop for such "small" cosmic objects. Amazingly, though, a 100-watt light bulb produces twice as much light-energy per unit of area as a Seyfert galaxy, which means that Seyferts achieve their brilliance by maintaining a rather moderate luminosity over an immense area.

Crowded Centers

Centers of some violently active galaxies are believed to be extremely dense, with billions of stars in a relatively small cosmic space. Seyfert galaxy NGC 4151, for example, one of the most intensely studied Seyferts, may have 10 billion stars in a relatively small cosmic space, with a diameter of 12 light-years (71 trillion miles, 114 trillion kilometers). This means that these stars, if distributed evenly, would be separated by distances equal to about ten times the distance to Pluto (37 billion miles; 59 billion kilometers), while the nearest star system to our Sun, Alpha Centauri, is seven thousand times the distance to Pluto. A planet situated in the center of this crowded star population but as far away as possible from any single star, would have a temperature similar to Earth's— though warmed solely by starlight. The brightest stars in this planet's sky would be about as bright as the full Moon, but the light would come from a pinpoint in the sky, not from a disk like the Moon.

Three exposures of Seyfert galaxy 4151—1 minute, 4 minutes, and 12 minutes. It is only the longer exposures that bring out the halo of stars surrounding the active, highly visible nucleus. This "fuzz," composed of billions of stars, has been found around distant quasars in recent years, and many astronomers are now convinced that quasars were at the center of young galaxies in the early Universe. *Courtesy Dr. William Morgan and Yerkes Observatory.*

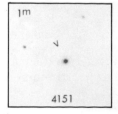
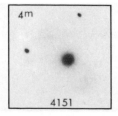
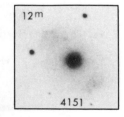

The Infrared Seyfert

Seyfert galaxies as a group emit strong infrared radiation from their cores, and Seyfert M77 currently holds the record as the most prodigious source of this kind of electromagnetic radiation, which lies between the radio and the visible bands of the spectrum. Seyfert M77's nucleus produces enough infrared radiation to equal the light energy from the 100-billion-plus stars in our galaxy. More amazing is the fact that this enormous infrared energy can switch on and off in just a matter of months, indicating that the core source is only about three hundred times the size of our solar system—just a cosmic speck, not even one twenty-fifth the distance to the nearest star in our Milky Way.

The Fast Seyfert Clouds

Near the cores of Seyfert galaxies are vast clouds of extremely hot gas at temperatures of 20,000 degrees Celsius—much hotter than in the core of our Sun. These clouds move outward, accelerated to high velocities by the central energy source, which data indicate is a gigantic black hole with a mass of millions of Suns and whose accretion disk is so overloaded with infalling material that the area heats up tremendously. This condition could propel some of the hot gas outward at high speeds.

Seyfert galaxy NGC 4151 has expanding gas clouds that travel at speeds of up to 17.9 million miles (28.8 million kilometers) per hour. If these hot clouds of gas were ejected from our Sun, they would take just over 5 hours to cover the 93-million-mile distance and reach the Earth's atmosphere. When they arrived, they would trigger violent magnetic storms, severe interruptions of radio and other communications, and dramatic and colorful displays of the aurora.

At the Heart of a Seyfert

The much studied Seyfert galaxy NGC 4151, in the constellation Canes Venatici, opened up its heart to astronomers

Many astronomers consider Seyfert galaxies such as M77 (NGC 1068) and NGC 1275, shown here, to be aging quasars that are closer to us in space and time. Seyfert M77 is one of the most powerful infrared sources known in the Universe. Its "small" nucleus, no more than three hundred times the size of our Solar System, gives off more infrared energy than our entire galaxy. *Courtesy Lick Observatory;* a Palomar Observatory Photograph. *Courtesy California Institute of Technology.*

in the late 1970s. An orbiting ultraviolet telescope made observations of this Seyfert's energetic center and found the radiations of carbon and magnesium in the data of their wavelengths. During the observations, this galaxy's nucleus flared up violently and gave the astronomers a rare opportunity to learn about what was going on in the central maelstrom. As the observations continued, the carbon light flared about two weeks after the initial flare, and then the magnesium light flared about two weeks later. By using the speed of light as a cosmic yardstick, the astronomers determined the distances of the carbon and magnesium clouds from the center of the Seyfert. By reckoning the distances from the center and by determining the velocities of the clouds through the blurred wavelengths of the carbon and magnesium, the astronomers had good observational data with which to calculate the mass of the object in the Seyfert's heart.

The central object's mass turned out to equal 100 million Suns, and it was contained in a volume of space not much larger than many stars! What could it be? You've guessed it. Astrophysical theory has only one answer: a massive black hole that gobbles up all matter that falls past its gravitational boundary, the event horizon. And astronomers ask, If Seyfert galaxy NGC 4151 contains a giant black hole at its heart, are there not millions of other galaxies—perhaps even our own Milky Way—that have these powerful gravity whirlpools at their centers? Before New Year's Eve of the year 2000 is celebrated, our instruments may be giving us closer views of these cosmic engines that guzzle stars and planets and great clouds of gas and take them forever out of our Universe.

The Quasar Future

Why do quasars increase dramatically in numbers as our instruments probe the depths of space and time, and then just as suddenly thin out and become rare again? No one knows for sure. While scientists are beginning to understand that quasars play a major role in the evolution of galaxies, they do not know much about what came before the quasars in the early Universe.

Seyfert galaxy NGC 4151 is one of the most intensely studied objects of its type. In recent years, astronomers have discovered a massive object at the center of its nucleus equal to 100 million Suns —a giant black hole that is capable of gobbling up stars whole. A Palomar Observatory Photograph. *Courtesy California Institute of Technology.*

How the quasars and galaxies formed in the early Universe is still a mystery to astronomers. This painting by space artist David Egge depicts the superpowerful quasars as they may have appeared a few million years after the Big Bang. *Courtesy David Egge,* © *1979.*

The Hubble Space Telescope and the proposed Advanced X-ray Astrophysics Facility will help fill in this blank in the history of the Universe by collecting data on the early evolution of quasars and what may have come before they turned on their powerful beacons during the early millennia of the Universe. Because the light we see from most quasars is billions of years old, we can only study their past and learn what they have probably become in the more recent Universe, but never in the present Universe. In today's Universe, these cosmic mysteries are extinct except for their ancient images traveling at the speed of light across vast expanses of space and time.

CHAPTER 5

THE UNIVERSE AT LARGE

The universe is not only queerer than we imagine, it's queerer than we can imagine.

J. B. S. Haldane
British geneticist

The Heavy Universe

The known Universe "weighs" about

10,000,000,000,000,000,000,000,000,000,000,000,000,-
000,000,000,000 tons—

that is, ten trillion trillion trillion trillion tons (10^{49} tons). A 36,000-ton ocean liner has a similar proportionate weight to the Sun as the Sun has to the entire Universe.

The Hierarchy of Matter

Active matter at the local level of the Universe is organized in single stellar systems, including their planets, and groups of stars in mutual gravitational attraction. Galaxies, with their billions of stars, are the next higher on the universal pecking order. They are the largest individual structures in the Universe. Larger still are the clusters of galaxies; the mean content of a cluster is about five galaxies, but some-

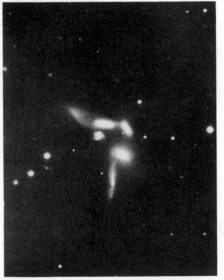

Galaxies, with their tens of billions of stars, are the largest individual structures in the Universe, and they travel through space and time in groups and clusters. Here are two small groups of four and five galaxies in the constellations Leo and Serpens. A Palomar Observatory Photograph. *Courtesy California Institute of Technology.*

times they have as many as a thousand members. While a debate continues, some experts believe that superclusters of galaxies are the intermediate hierarchical level of matter in the Universe. Dimensions from 150 million light-years to 300 million light-years are suggested for this level of organization. Finally, vast strings of galaxies appear to be the largest structural formation visible in the Universe—filaments throughout space and time.

The Neighborly Ellipticals

The densest, richest clusters of galaxies, often with thousands of members, appear to be composed of extremely bright elliptical or spherical galaxies. The center of such a massive group often has a concentration of galaxies centered around a supergiant elliptical galaxy with an immense halo of matter and a very active nucleus that emits powerful radio and other electromagnetic radiation.

Some astronomers have suggested that this might be the result of galactic cannibalism on an immense scale.

How Dense Is
Deep Outer Space?

The density of outer space is about one hydrogen atom per cubic inch, or about one atom for each two to three cubic centimeters. This is about 600 billion trillion times (6×10^{23}) less dense than water—600,000,000,000,000,000,000,000 times less dense. Got it?

As Many Stars
as Grains of Sand?

Are there more stars in the Universe than there are grains of sand on our planet Earth? Calculations have given us the answer to this question, and it provides an example of numbers invalidating well-known quotes.

There are, the number people tell us, more grains of sand on Earth than there are stars in the cosmic realm. Still, no one has made a physical count. To do so would take the entire population of planet Earth, 5 billion human beings, some 60,000 years.

How many stars in the Universe? No one really knows, because there is no way of physically seeing and counting them all. Not even the stars in our home galaxy, the Milky Way, have been precisely tallied. Even scientific estimates require assumptions based on the available evidence. Calculations are then built upon these assumptions. Here is how astronomers (in very general terms) estimate the number of stars in the Universe.

First, they take the estimated number of stars in an average galaxy: 100 billion (100,000,000,000, or 10^{11}). Next they take the estimated number of galaxies in the Universe: 1 trillion (1,000,000,000,000, or 10^{12}). Then they multiply the two values together. What is the bottom line? The estimated number of stars in the Universe is 100 billion trillion (100,000,000,000,000,000,000,000, or 10^{23}).

A Moving Parade

Any attempt to accurately estimate the number of stars in the Universe runs smack up against what is called the *parade effect.* Advertising executives face this problem all the time, because few audiences are fixed; groups of people are usually in constant change. It has been said that advertising does not try to reach a standing army, but tries to reach a moving parade. Astronomers attempting to precisely estimate the number of stars have the same problem, but it is magnified to a cosmic scale. Stars are always dying and stars are always being born. While there is now more observational evidence for dying stars—for example, the nova explosions and the number of white dwarf stars in our galaxy—than for newborn stars, this will dramatically change by the year 2000 because of the new astronomical observatories operating above Earth.

Astronomers tell us that perhaps as many as twenty new stars are born each year in the average galaxy. This means that the total number of new stars born in the Universe's 1 trillion galaxies each year could be 20 trillion. This is 55 billion new stars a day; 2.2 billion an hour; 36 million a minute, or 600,000 new stars created each second. Of course, the number of star deaths probably equals the number of star births; at least no serious astronomer is talking about overpopulation of the cosmos. The parade goes on; some of its stars drop out and new stars take their place. This has been going on for about 15 billion years.

Hydrogen, Hydrogen Everywhere

If all the matter in the Universe—galaxies, stars, interplanetary gas clouds and dust, planets, moons, and all of us—were spread out evenly over the immense, all-but-empty cosmic gulfs, there would still be one hydrogen atom in every 295 cubic feet (8.35 cubic meters) of space. And don't forget us: of every hundred atoms of living matter, about fifty are atoms of hydrogen. Our bodies are fuller of hydrogen than anything else.

The Universe: Less than a Googol

The number of atomic particles (electrons, neutrons, and protons) in the Universe is about 10^{80} or 100 million trillion trillion trillion trillion trillion trillion (the number 1 followed by eighty zeros). This staggering number still falls short of a googol, which mathematicians define as the number 1 followed by one hundred zeros, or 10^{100} (10 to the hundredth power). Still, the 10^{80} atomic particles in the Universe remains impressive, because their total represents one of the largest real numbers in the Universe—even if it is less than a googol.

Cold Today, with
Chance of Flurries

The average temperature of matter in today's Universe is about the same as the cosmic background radiation temperature: 2.7 degrees Kelvin (−270.3 degrees Celsius, −454.54 degrees Fahrenheit). This is the temperature of interstellar cyanogen found to be in thermal equilibrium with the background radiation. Any matter in the Universe, if far enough away from the stars, will be at the average temperature—until a supernova dramatically changes local weather conditions.

Hiking the Universe

If the expanding Universe we live in is closed, it will halt and collapse in the distant future. Its size (radius) today has been estimated at 104 billion trillion miles (167 billion trillion kilometers) in extent. That is:

104,000,000,000,000,000,000,000 miles
   or
167,000,000,000,000,000,000,000 kilometers.

A person setting out to hike today's Universe would have to plan on its taking at least 4.7 billion trillion years. But that is for only one way in a Universe that is always getting larger.

The Universal Merry-Go-Round

Do all objects in the Universe rotate? Clouds of interstellar matter that form stars rotate. All stars spin, including our Sun. Everything we see in our solar system rotates. And all galaxies, great and small, are carousels of the cosmos.

The rotation of cosmic objects smaller than galaxies can be explained by the collisions of gravitationally bound particles in the developing clouds of dark, and eventually hot, matter. The spin observed in galaxies, however, presents a fundamental problem for cosmologists. If the Universe began with a single bang, outward straight-line motions of the larger clumps of matter in the Universe can be explained. But circular motion?

It has been suggested that the entire Universe is rotating, thereby imparting some of its motion to the galaxies. Many, if not most, astrophysicists, however, believe that the observed motion can be explained by taking into account the behavior of the smallest particles and even the free subatomic particles. In this theory, as in the one for interstellar clouds, collisions between the innumerable tiny bits of mass that make up a galaxy's total weight add up to rotary motion. A dizzying prospect.

The Galaxy Lineup

If we could visualize a galactic police lineup, what would it look like? The smallest galaxy might weigh as much as 100 million Suns. The very largest would equal 1 trillion Suns or more. The big guys, then, can be ten thousand times the size of the smallest members of the galactic gang. This is like comparing a 40-pound (18-kilogram) dog to a 2-ton baby elephant.

We've Got Plenty of Nothing

The *Einstein Observatory,* an orbiting X-ray satellite, has allowed researchers to gain new knowledge about the matter between the stars and galaxies. This matter takes two forms: gas clouds and murky clouds of interstellar dust grains. The dust-grain regions block light and other radiation and thereby give away their presence. When distant X-ray sources are observed, the dust does what high-flying, frosty cirrus clouds do in our atmosphere: it causes halos to appear around the astronomical sources being imaged. The curious thing about these halos is that they cannot have been caused by all-the-same-size dust grains.

A group of scientists worked out formulas that suggest the average size of interstellar grains is about 0.1 micrometer (1/10,000 of a millimeter; or about 1/250,000 of an inch). What is the density of these grains within their clouds? The astronomers estimate about one grain per hundred cubic kilometers. If a large steamer trunk were filled up with the interstellar space from such dust clouds and carted to a laboratory for closer examination, how many trips would have to be made before there was a reasonable assurance of finding an actual interstellar dust speck?

Sit down, because you will need all the rest you can get before starting. The answer: 500 billion trips. And virtually every one of those trunks would be jam-packed with absolutely nothing!

The Composition of Almost Nothing

What do scientists think these interstellar dust grains are made of? They are probably made of two things: graphite grains ranging from 0.005 to 1 micrometer (1 micrometer = one thousandth of a millimeter or 1/25,000 of an inch; and "silicate"-type grains, ranging in size from 0.025 to 0.25 micrometer in size. This so-called silicate could be made of the minerals olivine, silicon carbide, iron, or magnetite.

Drawing the Universe

Want to draw a basic to-scale picture of the Universe? Here is how you can draw a slice of the large-scale Universe as astronomers observe and understand it today. Remember that this drawing will represent the largest structures in the Universe; it will not include our Sun and the planets, nor will it include our Milky Way Galaxy. Why? Because it would be impossible to represent them to scale; they would be far too tiny to include and still be seen with the human eye.

First, get two sheets of standard typewriting paper

(8$1/2$ × 11 inches will do). Then tape them together end to end with transparent tape and lay them out so that their longest dimension is horizontal. Get a pencil and sharpen it to the finest point possible. Now you are ready.

Carefully place a dot about $1/2$ inch from the right edge of the sheet. This point represents our Local Group of galaxies, which may be about 10 million light-years in diameter. Our Milky Way is about $1/100$ the diameter of this point. If four such dots can be placed side by side within $1/16$ of an inch, then the scale is about right. As you draw this slice of Universe, keep in mind the general scale: each $1/16$ of an inch equals about 50 million light-years.

Place another tiny, fine dot to the left of the one representing the Local Group's galactic family. This represents the next-nearest cluster of galaxies, the M81 Group, in the constellation Ursa Major, about 7 million light-years from our Solar System. Next, in the same direction, toward the center of the paper, place a third dot about $1/32$ of an inch from the first point. This represents the next-distant group, the M101 cluster of galaxies, also in the constellation Ursa Major. They are about 15 million light-years from us. In the direction of the upper edge, place a larger dot about $1/32$ of an inch from the original Local Group point. This represents the Virgo cloud of some twenty-five hundred galaxies, which are estimated to be 20 to 30 million light-years from our Solar System.

Is your pencil still sharp? If so, continue filling in the galaxies toward the left-hand edge with dots or short lines representing strings of galaxies. The largest string, about 1 billion light-years long, could be represented by a wavy line 1$1/2$ inches long, one third the distance to the left-hand edge. Two thirds of the way to the left end of the connected paper sheets, the galaxy clusters begin to thin out. The most distant galaxy known is located about 18$1/2$ inches from the Local Group's dot on this scale, which represents a distance of about 14.7 billion light-years.

A scattering of bright quasars can be sprinkled on the drawing with a flare pen or colored pencil, even though the dots will be much larger than actual scale of the small, powerful objects. The closest quasar is about 4 1/2 inches from the Local Group dot. This represents quasar 3C 273, in the constellation Virgo, some 3 billion light-years from us and the most distant object that can be seen through an amateur telescope with about a 10-inch mirror. At the distance of the most distant galaxy you have plotted, most of the points would be quasars. Between 18 1/2 inches and the far edge of the second sheet of paper is a zone of darkness, which represents an era in which no quasars are visible. This location in the Universe is so distant, and remote in time, that we can detect nothing with present instrumentation. Our hope is with the Hubble Space Telescope, which will soon bring the Universe closer to Earth.

The very edge of the paper opposite the Local Group represents the edge of the visible Universe. There, as everywhere, is the microwave background radiation from the Big Bang. The temperature of this radiation is 2.7 degrees Kelvin (-270.3 degrees Celsius; -454.5 degrees Fahrenheit). When astronomers "observe" the background radiation with radio telescopes, they are "seeing" the edge of the Universe. The microwave background radiation is actually our last look at the surface of the fireball at the beginning of our Universe.

Galaxy Habitats

Certain types of galaxies show certain preferences for their habitats. Allan Dressler, of Carnegie-Mellon University, has found that elliptical systems tend to gather where there is a greater overall density of galaxies. The spiral systems, according to Dressler, appear to prefer locations where there are fewer neighbors. This has helped astronomers predict what should be observed in certain regions of the Universe and thereby "strain out" nearby-foreground or distant-background objects.

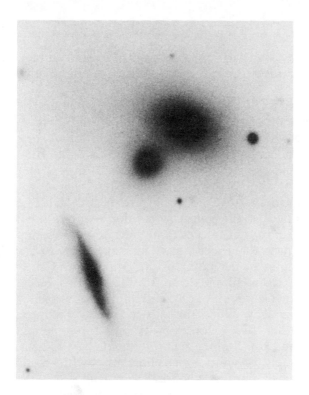

Astronomers can see more detail in negative prints such as this one. Here a pair of elliptical galaxies (top center) are believed to be colliding—more a collision of their powerful gravities than of individual stars, which miss one another by trillions of miles. *Courtesy Mark Hausman.* Reprinted from ***Mercury Magazine*** © 1979, Astronomical Society of the Pacific.

Galactic Cobwebs

What is the overall structure of our Universe? To the ancients, it was unchanging and Earth-centered. Then Galileo proved by actual observations what others had suggested: the Universe is vast. Later still, others noticed that the Milky Way had concentrations of stars in certain areas of the sky; this suggested that the Universe did indeed have a shape.

Edwin Hubble's work in the 1920s demonstrated that the "spiral nebulae" were actually external galaxies at great distances from our Milky Way, not just internal clouds of gas and dust, as some astronomers had thought. Hubble proposed that the galaxies were spread out evenly in all directions, but another astronomer, Harlow Shapley, at Mount Wilson Observatory, made an observational case that the distribution of the galaxies was not regular. Shapley conducted surveys of tens of thousands of galaxies, and the results showed that there was a "zone of avoidance" roughly at right angles to the plane of our Milky Way Galaxy. In response, Edwin Hubble demonstrated that this was because of the massive amounts of dust and diffuse interstellar matter in the Milky Way. When this was taken into account, Hubble proved that the Universe is isotropic—the same in all directions—and this finding generally holds true today.

A slightly symmetrical character to the cosmic background radiation, a radio fossil from the Big Bang, is now believed to be caused by our Milky Way Galaxy and presumably some of its neighbors in the Local Group, falling toward the giant Virgo cluster of galaxies at the rate of about 275 miles a second (almost 1.6 million kilometers an hour). The Virgo supercluster is an immense grouping of galaxies in the Universe that may be more than 1 billion light-years across.

While matter in the Universe does appear to be equally spread out in all directions at its very large scale, there is growing evidence that it is gathered in gigantic filaments with large gaps between strands. This has been likened to a three-dimensional cobweb or to Swiss cheese.

These immense filaments are composed of strings of galaxies and clusters of galaxies. Two astronomers from the University of New Mexico, using the 84-inch (2.1-meter) telescope at Kitt Peak National Observatory, near Tucson, Arizona, found the largest string so far observed, in 1985.

This cosmic cord of galactic knots is in the constellations of Perseus and Pegasus, the Winged Horse. It is estimated to be more than 1 billion light-years long. The astronomers were even able to plot it in three dimensions, and they think that it begins some 200 million light-years away from our galaxy and trails off at more than 1.2 billion light-years. For now, this can be considered the largest known organized structure of matter in the Universe.

If a light-year were scaled down to 1 foot (0.3 meter), then a person could walk the length of this string of galaxies by walking around the Earth at the equator 8 times. At the same scale, the nearest star, Proxima Centauri, would be within arm's reach. And, of course, at this scale, we would be giants several light-years tall!

The Giant Supercluster in Hercules

As astronomers connect clusters of galaxies to other clusters of galaxies by determining their common speeds of recession at certain distances, they uncover superclusters of galaxies.

The giant supercluster in the constellation Hercules is truly one of the largest cosmic structures known and includes three large galaxy clusters: Hercules, Abell 2151, and Abell 2199. The Hercules supercluster lies about 700 million light-years away, which means that if the diameter of our solar system were represented by 1 inch (2.54 centimeters), the Hercules supercluster would be 9.7 million miles (15.5 million kilometers) away—about equal to 20 round trips to the Moon. The extent of this supercluster is estimated to be 350 million light-years across space, covering 30 degrees of the Earth's sky, which is equal to sixty Moons lined up. Even though this area of light is too faint for human eyes to detect, it is still spreading onto the Earth's surface every day after its journey of 700 million light-years, which began before there were any plants, fish, reptiles, or people on planet Earth.

Coma and the Cosmic Net

Overhead in the springtime sky, in the constellation Coma Berenices, lies the famous Coma cluster of galaxies, invisible to the unaided eye. At least a thousand galaxies have been counted in this spherical cluster, all of which are about 400 million light-years away. Astronomers have measured the velocities of many of the galaxies in this cluster, and some are speeding within the cluster's gravitational bounds at over 2.2 million miles (3.6 million kilometers) per hour. Such high velocities mean a tremendous total mass for all the galaxies in the cluster, a mass that astronomers cannot find in the galaxies alone. Since this is the "brightest" X-ray-emitting cluster of galaxies known, however, an explanation comes forth for the missing mass—that there exists a thin, hot intergalactic gas throughout the cluster, a gas that is heated to a few million degrees Celsius as the galaxies (and their own gases) plow through it and create friction. The X-rays, detected by above-the-Earth telescopes like the *Einstein Observatory*, are emitted by this extremely hot gas.

The gravitational bounds of the Coma cluster were set at about 20 million light-years (two hundred times the diameter of our Milky Way Galaxy) for many years. But more extensive red-shift measurements in the 1970s told astronomers that some galaxies associated with the Coma cluster are at least 100 million light-years (a thousand times our galaxy diameter) away from the cluster's center. Another supercluster— the Coma supercluster—had been discovered. Knowledge of superclusters is helping astronomers understand the hierarchy of matter in the Universe. Evidence suggests that the Universe has a cellular structure, in which the clusters of galaxies are found in even larger, irregular structures—the superclusters—which are separated from one another by immense voids. The Coma cluster, it appears, is just a wispy strand in the filament of a vast cosmic net of interwoven superclusters.

The Hercules cluster of galaxies is believed to be a part of a super-cluster in the constellation Hercules, one of the largest cosmic structures known. It is about 700 million light-years away. If the diameter of our Solar System were scaled down to 1 inch (2.54 centimeters), then this supercluster (on the same scale) would be 8.7 million miles (14 million kilometers) away. A Palomar Observatory Photograph. *Courtesy California Institute of Technology.*

Another cluster of galaxies (known as Abell 1060), in the southern hemisphere. Some clusters contain more than a thousand galaxies. *Courtesy the Anglo-Australian Observatory,* © *1977.*

A large cluster of galaxies in the constellation Coma Berenices is part of a larger supercluster, which in turn is part of a vast cosmic net of interwoven superclusters—the texture of the Universe. *Courtesy National Optical Astronomy Observatories; Cerro Tololo Inter-American Observatory.*

These faint galaxies in Coma Berenices are barely visible, even with a long exposure time through the giant, 200-inch (5-meter) telescope at Hale Observatories. The white lines must be used to mark the positions of these faint, faraway galaxies. A Palomar Observatory Photograph. *Courtesy California Institute of Technology.*

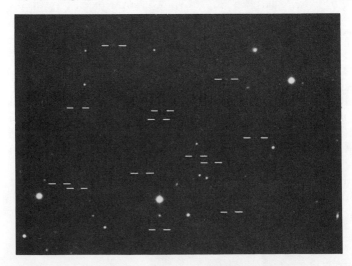

Cannibal Galaxies

At the centers of dense (astronomers call them "rich") clusters of galaxies there are always one or two supergiant elliptical galaxies. This is true of the Coma cluster, with the two brilliant giants NGC 4874 and 4889 situated at the bottom of the cluster's gravitational well. Many other galaxies at Coma's center are swarming around these giants, especially NGC 4889, and they appear to be heading toward a gravitational whirlpool. Indeed they are, and that is how the giants have grown so enormous—by cannibalizing the other galaxies in the cluster!

The dense galaxy cluster Abell 2199 also has a supergiant elliptical at its center, NGC 6166, a galaxy that easily dwarfs our Local Group's great Andromeda. Photographs of its nucleus reveal several components, what astronomers call "multiple nuclei," a feature that about half the supergiant elliptical galaxies have in common. In effect, supergiant NGC 6166 probably has been caught in the act of eating other galaxies, and its digestion of their cores is a slow process. But eventually, in a few hundred million years, the cores of the victims will be completely absorbed, and several galaxies will have become one.

In a few billion years, astronomers will see fewer galaxies in all, but there will be more brilliant supergiant cannibals, getting fat at the heart of dense clusters and left with only weak, dim, unattractive neighbors.

The Local Supercluster

The hierarchy of the Universe apparently does not end with great clusters of galaxies such as Virgo. Recent research in galaxy distribution (yes, there are specialists in this area of astronomy) indicates that the Virgo cluster may only be the concentrated core of an even more immense supercluster of galaxies that includes our own Local Group at one edge (again, we seem to find ourselves on the cosmic outskirts). This vast, flattened cloud of island universes may contain as

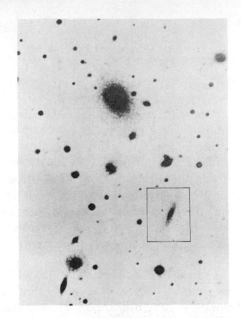

At the center of a dense galaxy cluster called Abell 2199 is a supergiant elliptical galaxy: NGC 6166. This enormous galaxy dwarfs our Local Group's great Andromeda (see inset, which is to scale). This negative print shows the fuzzy outer star regions. *Courtesy Mark Hausman.* Reprinted from ***Mercury Magazine*** © 1979, Astronomical Society of the Pacific.

The central region of the supergiant galaxy 6166 shows four components, probably smaller galaxies that it is digesting, earning a reputation as a cosmic giant cannibal. *Courtesy Mark Hausman.* Reprinted from ***Mercury Magazine*** © 1979, Astronomical Society of the Pacific.

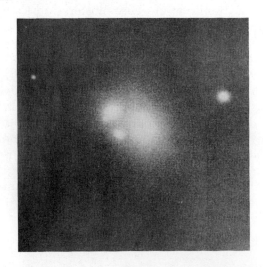

many as a hundred small groups which together contain
more than ten thousand individual galaxies. While the
smaller galaxy groups such as our local one and the central
Virgo cluster are bound together gravitationally, the entire
Virgo supercluster is not, but is, rather, expanding along with
the Universe. Also, the entire Virgo supercluster may rotate
over hundreds of millions, perhaps billions, of years.

The dimensions of this Local Supercluster, whose center
is the Virgo cluster, may have a diameter of 200 million light-
years. On a scale on which each light-year equals 1 inch (2.54
centimeters), the Local Group would have a diameter of 79
miles (127 kilometers), and the Local Virgo Supercluster
would have a diameter of almost 3,200 miles (5,150 kilometers). Scaling down even further for a size comparison, think
of a U.S. quarter dollar at the edge of a round table with a 40-
inch (102-centimeter) diameter, and you have an approxi-
mate size relationship between our Local Group of galaxies
and the Local Supercluster, which is centered on the Virgo
cluster.

A Cluster of Giants

The Virgo cluster of galaxies is the nearest large one to
our galaxy and its local neighbors. Estimated to be about 70
million light-years away, it is irregular in shape, as opposed to
the spherical shape of many more-distant clusters of galaxies.
For a vague idea of its immensity, even at our distance, which
is thirty-two times greater than that to Andromeda, hold out
an average-size book (about 6 × 9 inches, 15 × 23 centimeters) at arm's length. The book will just about cover the area
of the Virgo cluster in the sky, which has a diameter of over 5
million light-years.

Some 2,500 galaxies have been counted in the Virgo
cluster. Since an average galaxy contains about 50 billion
stars (an average of the giant and dwarf galaxies), this means
that the Virgo cluster may contain upward of 125 trillion
stars, a number 25,000 times Earth's human population.

Some Faraway Paces

The clusters and superclusters of galaxies are all flying away from us, taking part in the general expansion of the Universe. The Virgo cluster is casually moving away at 2.7 million miles (4.3 million kilometers) an hour; the Hercules cluster is cruising at 24.1 million miles (38.7 million kilometers) per hour; the Boötes cluster is speeding off at 86.4 million miles (139 million kilometers) per hour; and the Hydra cluster is really flying: 136 million miles (219 million kilometers) per hour. At Hydra's cosmic pace, a person with a life span of seventy years could make 3,546 circumnavigations of our solar system or 292,000 round trips to the planet Mars. For the stay-at-homes, there would be time for 3.3 billion trips around the Earth.

The Voids Between
the Clumps

Just as there are vast clumps of matter spread throughout the Universe (the galaxy superclusters), there are also vast voids between these cosmic clumps. When astronomers point their instruments toward the superclusters of Coma, Perseus, or Hercules, they see great voids in front of them. The Hercules supercluster's void is enormous: 330 million light-years deep. What would people see if they found themselves in the middle of this cosmic void? Nothing. If the nearest galaxies were over 100 million light-years away, the sky would seem black to the human eye. Only with a good telescope could one see the faintly glowing haze of distant galaxies. While there might be some isolated stars or globular clusters that had escaped from their former associations, there would be so few of them that they would appear no brighter than the distant galaxies that are invisible to the human eye. These vast cosmic voids, to the human senses at least, are immensities of nothingness.

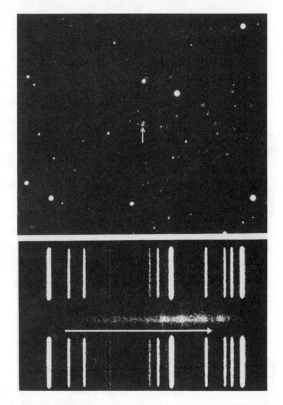

The red shift of light from the Hydra cluster of galaxies tells astronomers that they are flying away from us at 136 million miles (219 million kilometers) per hour—receding like everything else in our expanding Universe. At this speed, a person could fly around the world one and one half times every second. A Palomar Observatory Photograph. *Courtesy California Institute of Technology.*

Ultimate Cosmic Speeds

Distant galaxies and galactic clusters are receding from us and from other galaxies at tremendous speeds—all as a result of the cataclysmic Big Bang. The cluster of galaxies in the constellation Hercules is flying away from us at more than 20 million miles (32 million kilometers) per hour, but that is a turtle's pace compared to the speed at which the most distant galaxies and quasars known to science recede from us: 540 million miles (869 million kilometers) per hour, which approaches the speed of light (670 million miles per hour, over 1 billion kilometers per hour). At the speed of light a person could travel around the world 7 1/2 times in just one second.

How Smooth the Universe?

Galaxies are found in groups, clusters, superclusters, and long strings stretching across a billion or more light-years. Despite what might appear to be clumpiness in the organization of matter on these large scales, astronomers consider the Universe to be very smooth, taken as a whole at its very largest scale. The Universe has equal mass in all directions. It is homogeneous.

There does not appear to be a center, and theoretical predictions of the effects of an expanding Universe do not need a center—at least not in the traditional, observable sense.

The Universe is everything that ever was and ever will be, in all directions. And when we look at the Universe, it is everywhere as old as the beginning of time.

Prehistoric Radiation and the Transparent Universe

Is it possible to see backward almost to the beginning of time and actually see the Big Bang that began our Universe? Research in the 1940s predicted that the Big Bang's remnants might actually be detected, using the proper equipment, but confirmation of this theory waited twenty years.

In the early 1960s, two Bell Laboratories researchers, Arno Penzias and Robert Wilson, were working to identify and eliminate sources of interferences in satellite communications. From 1963 to 1965, they detected a mysterious microwave radiation with the giant horn-shaped radio telescope antenna at Holmdel, New Jersey. What was this signal and where was it coming from? It could not be attributed to any equipment they were using or other known sources. They did everything to eliminate the signal, and even cleaned pigeon droppings off the antenna. Still the mysterious signal persisted.

The curious radio noise they were detecting came from all directions in the sky and appeared to be unrelated to any Earthbound or individual celestial source. The radiation was equal to what would be emitted by a perfectly radiating body at a temperature of 2.7 degrees Kelvin above absolute zero (-270.3 degrees Celsius, -454.5 degrees Fahrenheit). This was calculated to be the radiation of the Big Bang fireball. It was moving away practically at the speed of light and was therefore shifted to the red end of the spectrum (the Doppler shift toward longer wavelengths) so that its original temperature of 3,000 degrees Kelvin appeared to be about a thousand times colder.

Penzias and Wilson soon learned that a group of researchers at nearby Princeton University were designing equipment that would search for the very fossil radiation they had found. The microwave radiation they observed was from the beginning of the Universe, remnants of the surface of the fireball at the beginning of time, just before it had cooled enough to allow the Universe to appear transparent and for atoms and matter to begin to form from the subatomic particles. For this work, Penzias and Wilson received the Nobel Prize for Physics.

The Paradox of the Night Sky

Why is the night sky dark? This child's question is one of the oldest questions in science, though to observers on Earth, the sky is never really dark. Even in the blackest desert or mid-ocean skies, there is a dim, diffuse glow from several sources. Airglow, brightest near the horizon, is from the recombination of molecules of air that have been ionized by sunlight during the day. The aurora is caused when air molecules in the upper atmosphere collide with charged particles from the Sun that have been trapped by the Earth's magnetic field. Then there is the sky glow from artificial illumination; astronomers call it light pollution. The background glow of stars and galaxies also makes its contribution to the light of the night sky.

The sky as seen from space, however, is incredibly dark. This has been confirmed by astronauts and cosmonauts in space, despite the glare on visors and windows caused by contaminants, the background star glow, and Solar System dust.

Why does the sky between the stars appear dark if the stars are almost everywhere, given enough space and time between us and them? Observations made with telescopes since the seventeenth century have shown that the telescopic sky is filled with stars. The more powerful the instrument, the more stars appear. Space is filled with stars. If a star's distance is doubled, its light will appear only one quarter as bright. However, at double the distance, four times the number of stars would be visible, and so they would radiate the same amount of light as the single star at the original distance, effectively doubling the total light visible. Each doubling of the radius observed should double the light visible—all the way to . . . infinity.

What if the more distant light is blocked by the intervening stars? The infinite brightness should be reduced to just the brightness of the surface of an average star such as our Sun.

The fact that the sky is not as bright as the surface of the Sun presents a remarkable paradox. This paradox, which assumed an infinite and unchanging universe, was first outlined by Jean Philippe de Cheseaux in 1744 and independently by Heinrich Olbers in 1826. It became known as Olbers' paradox—the paradox of the dark sky.

Olbers tried to explain the problem by suggesting that the Universe was filled with gas and was not a vacuum. There was a problem with this explanation, however. Such gas would be heated by the radiation from stars and would reradiate just as much energy as it absorbed. This obviously does not happen. Later explanations about how stars radiate and produce their enormous energy were also unsuitable.

It turns out that Olbers' paradox was finally explained by the new cosmology of the twentieth century. The Big Bang and the expanding Universe solves this classic astronomical riddle. As the light from distant galaxies and stars, racing away from each other and us, is shifted to the red end of the spectrum, it in effect loses some of its energy. Less light is therefore added to the sky than would otherwise be expected. The darkness of the night sky is another proof, along with the cosmic background radiation, that the Universe is expanding and that it began with the Big Bang.

The Now Universe

There is no way for anyone on Earth to know what is happening in the rest of the Universe now, right this second. It is impossible because of the speed limit of light and other electromagnetic radiation. Even the Sun's light is about $8^1/3$ minutes old when it reaches Earth. The farther out in space that astronomers and their technology peer, the older is that portion of the Universe they see or record. The now Universe is therefore unknowable, forever beyond human observation and knowledge. All astronomers can therefore be thought of as cosmic archaeologists, digging into the cosmic past in order to predict a future that may be beyond all human consciousness.

LIFE ABOVE EARTH

Extraterrestrial Life?

Speculation about life beyond our wet, blue-and-green Earth is not new. The Greek Democritus (c. 460–c. 370 B.C.) believed that innumerable Earths, peopled like our own, were spread across the cosmos. Metrodorus of Chios echoed these thoughts in the fourth century B.C., in his book *On Nature* when he wrote: "To consider the Earth as the only populated world in infinite space is as absurd as to assert that in an entire field sown with millet only one grain will grow." Nineteen centuries later, the Italian astronomer Giordano Bruno conceived of a Universe that extended to infinity, strewn with other suns and planets brimming with life. Bruno made the mistake of dabbling in politics and magic, and contradicted Church teachings. For this, he was burned at the stake in Rome in 1600. Only nine years later, Galileo Galilei found stars too numerous to count in his small telescope, and planets with orbiting moons of their own. A portion of Bruno's Universe was actually observed.

Today the idea of life beyond planet Earth is accepted by many, if not most, people. The possibility of life elsewhere in the Universe is acknowledged by the overwhelming majority of scientists. Public attitudes about extraterrestrial (ET) life have been fueled by the space programs of the superpowers, scientific pronouncements, and the cultural conditioning of books, movies, radio, and television. The real possibility of ET life has become an acceptable idea to millions of people in our late-twentieth-century culture.

There are, however, the doubters, and not all of them are so because of religious persuasion. Since the 1970s, a small but influential and growing number of scientists are having second thoughts about the inevitability of ET life. Their changing attitude is caused principally by the lack of evidence. They are also questioning some of the assumptions that have underlain the reasoning of the men and women who are proponents of life elsewhere in the Universe.

Are Extraterrestrials Visiting Earth Now?

Some people believe that the Earth is being visited, right now, by extraterrestrials or their robot emissaries, and that they travel to our planet in Unidentified Flying Objects. How realistic is this view? Not very. The so-called mystery of UFOs has been solved over the past twenty years.

What are the facts known about UFOs? First, there has never been a UFO or a proven artifact from a UFO recovered to study; there have only been *reports* of UFOs to study. Second, reviews of tens of thousands of reports by scientists, the military, the governments of virtually every industrialized country, as well as some pro-UFO researchers, have concluded that practically all sightings—98 or 99 percent—can be identified as commonplace occurrences, given enough time and information. Third, the number of unexplained sightings has turned out to be extremely small. All twenty or so inexplicable reports listed in the exhaustive 1968 University of Colorado Study of the U.S. Air Force files have now either been solved or serious questions have been raised about the facts in these cases. Fourth, in the highly emotion-charged atmosphere of UFO sightings, there does not seem to be such a thing as a genuinely reliable witness. People of all backgrounds—including technically trained pilots, engineers, and scientists—have reported things which upon investigation have turned out to be just unfamiliar or misidentified natural and man-made objects.

Fifth, the many ongoing scientific surveys of the night and day sky have produced no hard evidence to support the idea that UFOs are of extraterrestrial origin. These include the Smithsonian Astrophysical Observatory's Prairie Network, a ten-year survey by meteor cameras that covers the entire sky, military deep-space tracking radar with coverage out to tens of thousands of miles, and an estimated 800,000 hours each year devoted to observing the night sky by organized amateur astronomers.

What, then, are UFOs? Dr. Donald Menzel, the late director of Harvard College Observatory, enumerated 108 known, proven stimuli for UFO reports in his 1977 book *The UFO Enigma*. It is also clear that no evidence has come to light to suggest that the conclusions of the University of Colorado Study need be substantially updated: 29 percent of UFOs were astronomical objects, with Venus and meteors being the most common; 25 percent of the sightings were aircraft (in some locations, lighted advertising signs on planes or helicopters accounted for 20 percent); 18 percent were Earth satellites; 10 percent had other, miscellaneous causes such as birds or wind-blown pieces of paper; 8 percent had insufficient data for analysis; 4 percent represented balloons; 3 percent were proven hoaxes, and 1.9 percent remained unidentified. Later reviews of the Colorado and Air Force data by independent UFO researchers have trimmed down these unexplained sightings to even fewer "unknowns."

People no doubt see things in the sky for which they have no immediate explanation. But why are these thousands of observations, by people who are for the most part sincere and sober, interpreted by them as ET visitors from outer space? Can this really be the most logical or likely explanation for something seen in the sky that cannot be identified? How can they be so mistaken?

Unfamiliarity with the appearance of the phenomena of the sky, cultural conditioning (they expect to see UFOs), and wishful thinking certainly all play a part. More important is the well-known unreliability of unsupported eyewitness testimony, even by groups of people. Cornell astronomer Frank Drake, author of the famous Drake equation, describing the possibility of ET life, cites the experience of scientists searching for fallen meteorites from eyewitness accounts of fireballs —brilliant meteors that can cast shadows and lighten the night sky. According to Drake, interviewers found that 50 percent of the witnesses are wrong about facts after one day; 75 percent are wrong after two days; 90 percent are wrong after four days, and beyond five days most of the reports are more fantasy than fact. The implications of this witness reliability curve for UFO reports are obvious. Many people may want UFOs to exist and bring ET visitors to our planet, but there has not yet been one shred of compelling scientific evidence to prove they do.

Have ETs Visited
the Earth in the Past?

The notion that Earth has been visited by extraterrestrials in the past, and that there is evidence for such visits all around us, has been popular with many people in the past two decades. Popular writers have written bestsellers about this and nourished people's willingness to attribute many of humankind's accomplishments to magical, supernatural, or extraterrestrial forces. Tall tales have linked ET intervention to the construction of the pyramids; certain curious religious beliefs of African tribes, probably transplanted by European missionaries; huge figures designed on the South American deserts and visible from an airplane; alleged mutilation of livestock remains found in the southwestern United States; and rock formations of Mars akin to Vermont's Old Man of the Mountain.

The problem with such ideas is that all of them—be they on Earth or Mars—can be explained by mundane factors or coincidence; there is absolutely no need to evoke intelligent life from beyond our world for their explanation. There is no evidence today of ET visits in ancient rocks, in archaeological artifacts, or in old writings—no matter what the popularizers may say! On the other hand, it cannot be proved that visits have not occurred, particularly in the far distant past. As delightful and entertaining as some of these stories are, where is the scientifically acceptable evidence for such cosmic visits? We don't have it yet. But even the most diehard skeptics would love to find such evidence, would love to be proved wrong.

The Green Bank Account

We know for certain that life exists in the Universe. You and I are proof of it. But does it exist elsewhere? This is one of humankind's great unanswered questions.

Scientific attempts to reach some tentative conclusions about this ultimate question are largely twentieth-century efforts. One of the first and most influential attempts was begun in the early 1960s by Frank Drake, an astronomer at the Cornell Center for Radiophysics and Space Research. He developed what became known as the Drake equation, also called the Green Bank equation (Green Bank, Virginia, is the location of the radio telescope of the National Radio Astronomy Observatory, where Drake was working at the time).

In a simple formula, Drake tried to estimate the number of extraterrestrial civilizations. In $N = RPL$, N represents the number of civilizations, R equals the birthrate of new stars in our galaxy, P is the probability that a sufficiently advanced life-form will develop around that star, and L is the average life span of such a civilization. Using this formula, Drake and others arrived at an estimated 100,000 to 1 million societies that might be currently existing in the Milky Way.

Later, more elaborate versions of Drake's Green Bank equation were devised and used. An examination of the equation shows that the assumptions upon which the values R, P, and L are based are essential to estimating the possible occurrence of ET life within our galaxy or elsewhere in the Universe.

Each of these probabilities are multiplied with the others to arrive at the result. A glance at the more specific elements of succeeding versions of the equation shows the problem sharply:

- the average yearly rate of star birth in the Milky Way Galaxy
- the fraction of Sunlike stars that are single and not members of binary or multiple systems
- the number of Earthlike, habitable planets in each planetary system
- the fraction of planets on which life begins
- the fraction of life that evolves into "intelligence"
- the fraction of civilizations that have developed advanced technology
- the average lifetime in years of the civilizations with advanced technology.

Each element in the equation has its own underlying assumptions. Probably the one with the highest degree of accuracy is the rate of star formation within our galaxy—

estimated at about twenty stars per year. The least certain element is the number of technological civilizations. It could range from 1 (ours, the only one we know for certain) to millions.

A Million Worlds

The possibility of 1 million societies in the Milky Way Galaxy alone? Yes, this is the bottom line of the Green Bank account. Think of it—a million planets:

- around a million stars (some are young, like ours, and some are old and dying)
- a million intelligent species
- a million histories (consider what has been lost of the Earth's history)
- a million sunsets (if their planets spin as our Earth does, which is highly likely)
- 5 billion million bcings (or more or less)
- 500 million gods (or a million or one or none at all)
- a million seas (or is there water and if there is, could it be ice or vapor?)
- a million skies (where some strange rains no doubt fall)
- a million moons (or 2 million or 10 million)
- a million or many million ways to speak, to think of themselves, to love

The Eyes of a Bee

Our eyes see the stars, galaxies, and other celestial objects through a small and narrow window in the electromagnetic spectrum: visual light. Our daylight eyes see light that is essentially yellow-green in wavelength. This is called the photopic eye, the eye of the color-producing cone cells. The dark-adapted eye, the scotopic eye, distinguishes light that is slightly bluer. It uses the rod cells. If one speculates on the possible reasons for this difference in our species' ability to see, it makes common sense. After all, we have evolved around a yellow star; the Sun's energy output peaks in the yellow. At night, however, our eyes are most sensitive to the bluish green of deep twilight, a time of danger for animals. As a result of this curious dichotomy of sight, we cannot see much color when we view the naked-eye stars. They appear white to our eyes most of the time. Only the very brightest stars, mostly yellow or orange objects, transmit enough photons to show colors different from the rest.

What if humans had evolved around a star system with radically different spectral characteristics? Alternatively, what if we had radically different vision needs? We might have the ultraviolet sight of bees. Or our vision might peak in the infrared if we were around a star surrounded by a thick blanket of dust. If our planet had long periods of darkness and we needed to detect heat, infrared vision would also come in handy, as it does for certain snakes. Humans have just a vestige of the ability to see polarized light, a useful thing if it is important to know the direction people are going during migrations. Consider certain lizards such as the western fence lizard. It has a pineal gland (found buried deeply in the human brain) on the back of its head, equipped with a lens—a third eye.

Twentieth-Century Starships

We have already sent four spacecraft to the stars. In 1977, two American spacecraft were launched to the giant outer planets of our Solar System. Voyager 2 was sent to Jupiter, Saturn, Uranus, and Neptune; and Voyager 1 was launched to Jupiter and Saturn. Both spacecraft will eventually leave our Sun and Solar System behind.

In 1972 and 1973, the Pioneer 10 and 11 spacecraft were sent to Jupiter and Saturn to continue on an endless journey beyond the Solar System. Pioneer 10 became the first man-made object to leave our Solar System, in June 1983, traveling at a speed of about 25,000 miles (40,000 kilometers) per hour. At this rate, if Pioneer 10 were headed in the direction of Proxima Centauri, our closest known star neighbor (4.2 light-years away), the spacecraft would reach its destination in 112,000 years. As it is, this little emissary from Earth may pass close to a star system sometime within the next 10 million years.

If an Apollo spacecraft, like those that carried U.S. astronauts to the Moon nine times in the 1960s and 1970s, traveled at the average round-trip-to-the-Moon speed of about 3,300 miles (5,280 kilometers) per hour, it would reach Proxima Centauri in a mere 848,000 years.

Starship Daedalus

Voyages to "nearby" stars with present-day technology is clearly impossible, and this will hold true for the rest of this century. But will such a voyage even be possible in the next century? A thorough study done in the 1970s, Project *Daedalus*, by the British Interplanetary Society, is a tentative answer. It addresses the formidable technological challenges head on and does not gloss over the real problems of such a venture.

The Project *Daedalus* study deals with sending a robot starship, *Daedalus*, to Barnard's star, a small reddish dwarf star about 6 light-years away. The star probe would be propelled by a power source called a nuclear pulse rocket. This device would constantly explode marble-sized spheres of frozen deuterium and helium-3. Electron beams would explode these devices in the compulsion plant behind the spaceship, eventually providing the thrust necessary to reach a peak speed of about 13 percent the speed of light (86 million miles, 138 million kilometers, per hour). *Daedalus*, the Greek word for "cleverly wrought," would reach Barnard's star in about fifty years.

The payload of the starship would be about 400 tons (364,000 kilograms), or five times the weight of the U.S. Skylab space station. It would speed right by the star and release a swarm of seventeen instrumented probes.

Here is the hitch, however. The helium-3 fuel is practically nonexistent on Earth and would have to be either extracted from the atmosphere of Jupiter or bred on the surface of the Moon. The waste heat from this latter process on the Moon would equal the entire world's present energy consumption for a period of seven hundred years.

Brothers of the Sun

A survey of nearby stars like the Sun that could be visited by a robot starship like *Daedalus* were selected by the study team based upon distance, star type, temperature, life span, probability of planets, and probability of the evolution of life. Some of the stars listed below will probably be ports of call for starships from Earth in the next five hundred years.

Star (According to Rank)	Distance in Light-Years
Alpha Centauri A & B	4.3
61 Cygni A & B	11.2
Barnard's star	6
Epsilon Eridani	10.8
Tau Ceti	11.8
Proxima Centauri	4.2
Luyten 726-8 A & B	8.9
Wolf 359	7.5
Epsilon Indi	11.2
Sirius A & B	8.6
Lalande 21185 A & B	8.1
Ross 154	9.4
Ross 248	10.4

The Ultimate Search

The idea of extraterrestrial life has been a part of twentieth-century art and culture, especially so since the Moon Age began, in the 1960s. The serious scientific study and actual search with radio telescopes, however, is a relatively recent endeavor. In 1959 an early paper written by Giuseppe Cocconi and Philip Morrison, "Searching for Extraterrestrial Communications," appeared in the prestigious British science magazine *Nature*. A review of possible extraterrestrial search strategies in the paper showed that a radio search probably had the best chance for success. This can be considered the beginning of serious scientific work on the subject.

The search for life beyond our planet has taken several approaches. Nearby stars have been observed closely by Earth-based telescopes and spacecraft for signs of planetary systems. Manned and unmanned space exploration of our own solar system has included tentative investigation. Passive searches for communications from other galactic civilizations have been done over the past two decades, and future efforts will be more sophisticated and cover much more of the electromagnetic spectrum. One message has also been sent to a globular cluster of stars some 25,000 light-years away. Other researchers have considered the possibilities for the origin of life in deep space by studying the chemistry of interstellar clouds. This search for other life in the Universe, which began in the twentieth century, may well continue for hundreds, even thousands, of years without contact.

Ozma and the Radio Search

More than four dozen radio searches for extraterrestrial intelligence have been conducted since 1960. The first, Project Ozma (named after the princess of the Land of Oz) was the brainchild of Frank Drake. A 26-meter (86-foot) radio telescope was turned on the nearby Sunlike stars of Tau Ceti and Epsilon Eridani, and the equipment listened at the 21-centimeter wavelength. Radio searches, so far unsuccessful, now include sophisticated devices called multichannel spectrum analyzers, to observe many wavelengths simultaneously. Scientists in seven countries have participated in this work to date. The countries include the United States, the U.S.S.R., Australia, France, the Netherlands, the German Federal Republic, and Canada. Even the International Astronomical Union (the international organization of professional astronomers) gave legitimacy to the search for extraterrestrial intelligence in 1982 when it formed its Commission 51, "Search for Extraterrestrial Life." The IAU was urged to do so by a petition signed by more than seventy scientists from many nations, which included many Nobel laureates. While some myopic Earthlings such as U.S. Senator Proxmire may poke fun at such research, the activity represents what is best in humankind: the quest, the reach for knowledge and understanding.

The Cosmic Water Hole

How is it possible to narrow down the millions of possible transmission frequencies in the electromagnetic spectrum and choose one upon which we can eavesdrop? One frequency band that scientists consider a cosmic "radio quiet" zone is between about 1 and 10,000 megahertz. This falls between the noise from the cosmic background radiation of the Big Bang and the noise from the Earth's atmosphere. Within this range is a so-called magic frequency of the radiation emitted naturally by neutral hydrogen—the most common atom in the Universe. This frequency is 1,420 megahertz (1.4 gigahertz or 1.4 billion radio waves per second). But this is also a source of background noise, and so other scientists have suggested the frequency of the so-called hydroxyl radical—the combination of one hydrogen atom and one oxygen atom—at 1,662 megahertz.

It so happens that the addition of one hydrogen atom to another hydrogen atom and one oxygen atom creates water, H_2O. The range between these two frequencies has been suggested as a "natural" for civilizations wanting to communicate their presence. The first detailed engineering study of a system to detect intelligent life, known as Project Cyclops, called this magic frequency range the "Om and the Um . . . [which] beckon all water-based life to search for its kind at the age-old meeting place of all species: the water hole."

Lonely in the Solar System?

No conclusive evidence of the existence of other life within our Solar System has been found. In fact, most of the planetary bodies in our system are inhospitable to life-forms as we know them. Most of the moons in our Solar System are much like our own Moon: airless, waterless, and bombarded by powerful radiation. No evidence of life was found by the twelve U.S. astronauts and the three Soviet robot rovers that visited and brought back rock and soil samples from our Moon.

In 1976, two Viking spacecraft landed on Mars and conducted experiments that tested the Martian environment for life. While three of the experiments gave results suggesting that life might be present, a fourth concluded that there could be no life as we understand it. Despite this ambiguity, after several years of studying the results, the majority of scientists on the team conclude that there is no Martian form of life at the two Viking locations on Mars.

It has been suggested by some scientists, including the well-known astronomer Carl Sagan, that life could evolve in the atmosphere of Jupiter or Saturn, or maybe in the rich atmosphere of Saturn's large moon Titan. By the year 2100, we will be certain to know if life in any form lives elsewhere in our Solar System.

Planets Around Other Stars

Searches for planet-sized objects around nearby stars go back to the 1930s. Peter Van de Kamp, an astronomer working at Sproul Observatory, Swarthmore College, in Pennsylvania, and other researchers, have used long-focus nineteenth-century telescopes and newer instruments to measure the minute position changes of stars with large proper motions—that is, motion changes detectable over periods of a year or a few years from the various points along the Earth's orbit around the Sun.

Barnard's star, at a distance of 6 light-years, was the first candidate to be studied that Van de Kamp believed had unseen companions, too small to be stars, orbiting it. Since his announcement, in 1962, a number of other stars have been measured that show odd motions—perturbations, as the astronomers call them—including Van Beisbroeck 8, later believed to have a Solar-System-type cloud of dust surrounding it.

Until very recently, when state-of-the-art observational satellites joined the search, this work was highly controversial. Why? Because the observations were at the very limit of detection for many of the telescopes used. Also, much of the work at the Sproul Observatory was thrown into question because of an unfortunate setback. When the telescope was cleaned in the late 1940s, one of its large lens elements was slightly rotated when it was put back into place. When this was realized, several years later, all the data collected during that time had to be discarded, and the long period of observations, about twenty years, had to be started all over again.

Another method often used to search for planets beyond our Solar System involves measuring the Doppler shift of the dark spectral lines of nearby stars. These dark spectral lines result from absorption of the stars' light by matter in their outer atmospheres. If the lines are shifted to the red, it means the star is moving away; if toward the blue, the star is moving toward us. The spectra can also indicate a wiggle, and such a slight motion can be detected even if we are seeing a planetary system edge on. A detected wiggle, of course, may indicate the presence of an unseen companion.

But the most exciting promise for the search for distant planets, beyond our solar system, is the Hubble Space Telescope, which will search for planets from its clear-view orbital perch above the Earth.

The Hot Search

In 1983 the Infrared Astronomy Satellite (IRAS) surveyed the entire sky in the wavelengths given off by warm celestial bodies. More than seventy possible candidates for unseen objects orbiting nearby stars were found. One southern-sky star, Beta Pictoris, was actually found to have a flattened disk of materials surrounding it—possibly a "solar system" undergoing formation. Another star, Van Beisbroeck 8, earlier tagged by Peter Van de Kamp as a possible place for

A "solar system" in the making? Astronomers believe that planets may be forming around this southern-sky star, Beta Pictoris, which is 50 light-years away from Earth. The white disk of material visible on either side of the occulting mask device may already have given rise to primordial planets that may someday be a home for ET life. *Courtesy NASA.*

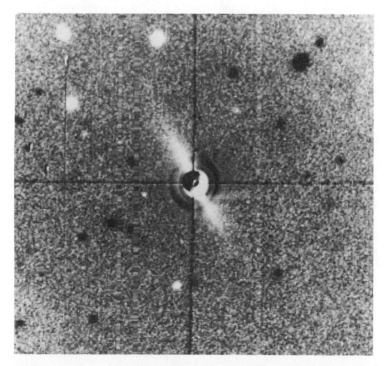

finding a planet, was observed to have a similar feature that indicated a "solar system." Later, astronomers at the University of Arizona's Steward Observatory and at Kitt Peak National Observatory, in Tucson, detected an object near the star VB 8 that was estimated to be five to fifty times the diameter of our giant planet Jupiter. This object, classified as a dark "brown dwarf," is theoretically too small to be a star. This computer-enhanced observation, however, was called into serious doubt in October 1986 when astronomers could no longer detect the object.

The IRAS satellite amassed a mountain of data which will be studied for years by astronomers of many specialties. Among these data, there may even be evidence of another planetary system awaiting discovery. Future infrared instruments on the drawing boards will be many times more sensitive than IRAS's sensors, and they may even be capable of imaging actual neighboring planets. Such an exciting prospect is less than a decade away.

Where Are They?

Most scientists who study the possibility of ET life believe that it quite probably, if not inevitably, exists elsewhere in the Universe. The lack of evidence is, however, disquieting.

The famous physicist Enrico Fermi is often cited as surprising his dinner companions at Los Alamos, New Mexico, one day in 1943. The talk turned to the possibility of ET life, and Fermi asked, "Where are they?" This became known as the Fermi paradox. If ET life exists, there should be evidence of it all around us.

One ET pessimist, Los Alamos scientist Eric Jones, has postulated that the presence of a technological civilization would be evident throughout our galaxy in less than 100 million years. Others make the case that this would happen in as little as 10 million years.

Several reasons have been given as to why we do not

have evidence of extraterrestrial life all around us. These reasons are all very speculative. First, perhaps ET life does not want to reveal itself to us. It is possible that a galactic civilization has decided that we are not safe or not that important. Or there may be no technological civilizations around to contact us. If this is true, there may be a sobering reason. It may be that technological civilizations do not last long, that they destroy themselves. Are we the only active technological civilization in our galaxy? That, too, is possible. We do not know if we will end up destroying ourselves.

Perhaps the 4 billion years or so it took our planetary system and civilization to evolve (this is the only example we have) is not enough time for most planets to form a hospitable environment for life, if they ever can.

If advanced galactic civilizations do exist, they may in fact be too intelligent to waste the great resources necessary to span the vast distances of space and time between the stars. The so-called quest motivation of humankind may not exist for ET life, or perhaps they have outgrown it. But as a species, we continue to hunt for other life in the Universe. As our hunting methods improve and become more sophisticated, our chances of receiving intelligent signals from ET life improve dramatically over time.

CHAPTER 6

THE PAST AND
FUTURE UNIVERSE

Now entertain conjecture of a time
When creeping murmur and poring dark
Fills the wide vessel of the universe.

—Shakespeare, *King Henry V*

The Big Bang Gang

Not even Albert Einstein could believe that the Universe was
expanding, all its galaxies and clusters of galaxies filled with
billions upon billions of stars flying away from one another,
and it took him fifteen years to admit, and others to point out,
that two expanding-Universe solutions could be found to the
equations in his General Theory of Relativity. It was with the
publication of this theory, in 1917, that Albert Einstein un-
wittingly began the Big Bang theory of the origin of the
Universe. His General Theory, more than any other work,
established modern cosmology. Other men amplified and
expanded on Einstein's work and its implications for cosmology. We can think of them together as the Big Bang gang.

First there was Vesto Melvin Slipher, an American astronomer working at the Lowell Observatory in Arizona.
While studying the Andromeda nebula (it was not then
known to be a stellar system external to the Galaxy), he
discovered that many nebulae (galaxies) were receding at
high velocities. By 1914, Slipher had found thirteen receding

galaxies. He did not appreciate the import of this discovery, but Edwin Hubble knew about his work and understood its significance. It was the first observational clue to the expanding Universe.

Willem de Sitter was a Dutch astronomer and cosmologist who did pioneering work in relativity theory. In 1917, after receiving a copy of Einstein's work, he found a solution to the equations that predicted an exploding Universe, one that was finite and unbounded (think of the surface of an expanding balloon). After World War I, this "de Sitter Universe" became well known among scientists and much discussed. De Sitter was also responsible for making Arthur Eddington, the famous English astronomer, aware of Einstein's and his own work.

Alexander Friedmann, a Russian mathematician, found another expanding-Universe solution to Einstein's theory, after he discovered a simple error in Einstein's math. Einstein, after some hesitation, acknowledged Friedmann's results as "correct and illuminating." A few years later, before he emigrated to the United States, George Gamow was Friedmann's student.

Georges Lemaître, a Belgian priest who was a student of Arthur Eddington's, discovered an expanding-Universe solution to Einstein's equations in 1927. His solution was found independently of Friedmann's, to which it was similar. He presented a giant "primordial atom" as the primary state of the Universe.

Arthur Stanley Eddington was the organizer and public relations man for the Big Bang gang, always keeping the theories and personalities flowing. He was also an outstanding astronomer and popular science writer, the latter efforts of which did much to publicize De Sitter's and Lemaître's work. He also knew of Hubble's work in the United States. Eddington spoke before the Royal Astronomical Society in 1930 and went on record as supporting Hubble's work and the expanding-Universe theory that resulted. He was the first to intuit the coming revolution in our knowledge of the Universe.

Edwin Hubble became the Big Bang gang's great ob-

The Big Bang gang, the men who discovered our Universe, from top left, going across: Albert Einstein in the back seat with the Galaxy expert, Harlow Shapley; Vesto M. Slipher; Willem de Sitter; Alexander Friedmann. Bottom left, going across: Georges Lemaître; Arthur S. Eddington; Edwin Hubble; and George Gamow. Credits: Einstein and Shapley, *courtesy MIT Historical Collection, Herald*

Traveler Photo, AIP Niels Bohr Library; Slipher, Eddington, and De Sitter, *courtesy AIP Niels Bohr Library;* Friedmann, *courtesy **Soviet Physics Vspekhi**, January 1964;* Lemaître, photo by Dorothy Davis Locanthi, *courtesy AIP Niels Bohr Library;* Hubble, *courtesy Hale Observatories, AIP Niels Bohr Library;* Gamow, *courtesy AIP Niels Bohr Library.*

server and collector of empirical evidence in the late 1920s, along with his colleague Milton Humason. Influenced by the work of Slipher and De Sitter, he also was fortunate to be working with the largest telescope in the world at the time: the 100-inch reflector (254 centimeters) at Mount Wilson. He was the first man in the world to prove that nebulae were really external island universes of billions of stars and not clouds of gas within our own stellar system. He also demonstrated the amazing velocity (red shift) / distance relationship between galaxies (the farther away, the faster they recede). He took the idea of the expanding Universe from theory to empirical data.

George Gamow, a Russian-born scientist who emigrated to the United States in 1933, modernized and upgraded Georges Lemaître's expanding-Universe theory and, in fact, coined the phrase "Big Bang theory." Gamow, like Eddington, saw the link between the Universe and the atom. During the 1930s and '40s, he and his colleagues Ralph Alpher and Robert Herman worked on the Big Bang theory of the creation of the elements. Out of their work came the theory in 1948 of the cosmic-fireball radiation and its remnant in the present-day Universe. It was discovered, as accidentally as Slipher's receding galaxies, in 1964 by Arno Penzias and Robert Wilson.

All the Big Bang gang members never met in one place together. A 1923 meeting in the Netherlands brought three of them together: Einstein, Eddington, and De Sitter. Eventually Einstein met Georges Lemaître, in 1927 in the United States, and a few years later, in 1931, he met Edwin Hubble at Mount Wilson, where he studied Hubble's plates and peered through the great, 100-inch telescope. After reviewing the evidence, Einstein admitted for the first time—a full fifteen years after his General Theory of Relativity was published—that it was likely that "the general structure of the Universe is not static." He finally accepted an expanding Universe and admitted to the worst mistake of his scientific career: he had earlier changed his equations because he could not accept the concept of an unstable, expanding Universe.

The dome and the interior of the 60-inch (152-centimeter) telescope on Mount Wilson, where Edwin Hubble began to map the Universe. *Courtesy California Institute of Technology Archives.*

In these fifteen short years (1917–32), humankind's knowledge of the Universe had expanded more than any other time in history—from one stellar system, the Galaxy, to millions; from an eternal, unchanging Universe to an exploding, expanding one. The Age of Discovery (1482–1522) and its four great explorers who led the way—Dias, Columbus, Da Gama, and Magellan—increased the area of the known world tenfold. The Big Bang gang, in just fifteen years, expanded the known Universe a trillionfold.

Hubble's Law and the Expanding Universe

Edwin Powell Hubble (1889–1953) was an American astronomer who worked with the largest telescopes in the world during his thirty-odd-year career—the 60- and 100-inch (1.5- and 2.5-meter) telescopes on Mount Wilson and later the 200-inch (5-meter) reflector on Palomar Mountain —and aimed them at the most distant objects known at that time. His astronomical work, while built upon that of others, represents the greatest leap in the understanding of the Universe since Copernicus. The Hubble Space Telescope, named in his honor, will take astronomy farther out in space and back in time than ever before.

Hubble demonstrated that the so-called spiral nebulae were vast and distant spiral galaxies, composed of millions of individual stars, outside the Milky Way Galaxy. This was his first major contribution, and he proved it with long-exposure photographs of the Andromeda Galaxy, which showed individual stars for the first time. Then he and his associate, Milton L. Humason, went on to measure the speeds and distances of faraway galaxies. These observations and statistics eventually led to Hubble's law, which revolutionized astronomy—and even proved that Einstein himself could let subjective values influence his equations and cosmology. Hubble's law states that there is a constant proportion between recession velocity of distant galaxies and their dis-

The 100-inch (2.5-meter) Hooker Telescope at Mount Wilson gathered the evidence of the Big Bang for Milton Humason and Edwin Hubble. Einstein peered through this instrument in 1931 when he visited Hubble at Mount Wilson. Einstein finally knew that the Universe was expanding, and admitted to the biggest mistake of his career. *Courtesy Mount Wilson and Las Campanas Observatories and AIP Niels Bohr Library.*

tance. Often referred to as the velocity/distance relationship, this was observational proof of the expanding Universe—the Universe is flying apart, and the Galaxy, the Solar System, the Earth, and we are part of the flying debris.

Hubble's Variable Constant

Hubble's constant is the rate at which the Universe's expansion velocity changes with distance. This quantity measures, in other words, how fast the Universe is expanding. The speed of a faraway receding galaxy is equal to its distance multiplied by Hubble's constant. Transposing the equation: the constant equals the faraway galaxy's velocity divided by its distance.

Astronomers over the past few decades have affectionately called this quantity Hubble's variable—not to detract from its cosmic validity, which has been demonstrated many times, but to point out the fact that it has been revised several times to reflect more sophisticated measurements of the extreme cosmic distances on which it depends for its value. Extreme distances are determined by measuring the faint light from galaxies that are billions of light-years away. Once the intrinsic brightness of a faraway galaxy is known, its distance can be calculated by observing how bright it appears to be.

The measurement of Hubble's constant is given as so many miles or kilometers per second for every 3.26 million light-years' distance (which equals a megaparsec). Hubble's initial value was ten times higher than its present value, mainly because the 100-inch (2.5-meter) telescope was bringing in images of a Universe never seen before, and experience had not yet adapted to technology. His value was about 372 miles (526 kilometers) per second for every 3.26 million light-years' distance. An often-used current value of Hubble's constant, one published by Allan R. Sandage and G. A. Tammann in 1975, is 34 miles (55 kilometers) per second for every 3.26 million light-years' distance.*

Thus Hydra, a remote cluster of galaxies that is almost 4 billion light-years away (the light observed is 4 billion years old!), is traveling at 136 million miles (219 million kilometers) per hour. This speed would take you on a one-way trip to the planet Saturn in just 6.5 hours or around the world over 5,000 times in just one hour.

---

* The value of Hubble's constant is still vigorously debated and studied. For the purpose of consistency and calculation, the above velocity value of 55 kilometers per second per 3.26 million light-years is assumed here.

Looking Back in Time with Cosmic Candles

In astronomy, a standard candle is not a slender, white taper of tallow, two of which grace a table's centerpiece at formal dinners. It is, rather, this science's designation for certain classes of celestial objects, usually stars or galaxies, that are believed to share a standard luminosity and are used to measure the Universe. Cosmic distances, along with velocities, give us Hubble's constant, which in turn tells us the expansion rate, the age, and perhaps eventually the destiny of the Universe.

The largest standard candle used in astronomy is the brightest galaxy in a cluster of galaxies—usually one of the supergiant elliptical galaxies that are centrally located in a cluster. The giant elliptical galaxy NGC 4889, in the rich Coma cluster of at least a thousand galaxies, is an example of one of these largest standard candles. It is estimated at about 391 million light-years away and can be used to determine even vaster cosmic distances by jumping to even more distant galactic clusters billions of light-years away to compare them with other supergiant galaxies. This giant galaxy is estimated to be more than 100 billion times brighter than the Sun, and just 1 square inch of the Sun is brighter than 300,000 dinner-table candles.

The Cosmic Distance Ladder

Astronomers, with their cosmic standard candles in hand, have been climbing the cosmic distance ladder for decades. It is a strenuous climb, *up and down.* The rungs are far apart and slippery, but views from the top and the bottom of this ladder may eventually present a clear view of the entire Universe—its birth, evolution, and destiny. Here is a progress report on the climb *up* the ladder to view the observable Universe.

Rung 1: Measurement of distance and luminosity of nearby stars by using triangulation, with the Earth–Sun distance and the Earth's orbit around the Sun as baselines. This allows determination of distance to star clusters in our galaxy, which contain variable stars called Cepheids.

Rung 2: Measurement of the intrinsic brightness of Cepheid-variable stars (stars that vary in brightness in a regular, predictable way). A Cepheid's variable period will tell its luminosity.

Rung 3: Measurement of distances to nearby galaxies by determining the luminosity of Cepheid stars in these galaxies.

Rung 4: Measurement of large clouds of hot gas in the nearby spiral galaxies by knowing their distance.

Rung 5: Measurement of the gas clouds in spiral galaxies still farther away and comparison of them with the gas clouds in nearby galaxies, which gives their distance. This takes astronomers out to 36 to 180 million light-years' distance.

Rung 6: Measurement of the average brightness of all spiral galaxies for which distances have been found.

Rung 7: Measurement of spectra and velocities (red shifts) of spiral galaxies many hundreds of millions of light-years away, which will give distances by knowing the average brightness of the closer galaxies.

Rung 8: Measurement of the velocities and distances of many faraway spiral galaxies will give a more precise value to Hubble's constant—one of the major keys to understanding the Universe.

Astronomers have recently put their first foot on Rung 8 and are beginning to see the Universe. The Hubble Space Telescope will soon be finding the next rung. No one really knows how many rungs the ladder has, and there is always the chance of a fall; after all, the rungs are slippery, especially when one climbs down to reach the unpredictable and still mysterious realm of quantum physics.

You see, this is a ladder that can be climbed up or down. If you climb up, as we just did, you will see the large-scale observable Universe of galactic clusters and quasars expanding outward, perhaps forever. If you climb down, you will reach the strange realm of micro space and micro time that goes beyond the realm of classical physics. This micro realm—where time and distance and mass are divided trillions and trillions of times into all but unimaginably small quantities and where everyday human experience has a heavy and dark door slammed in its face—is where many astrophysicists and theorists are today struggling to find the ultimate answers. What happened at the instant of the Big Bang? When was the exact instant of the Big Bang beginning? What happened before the Big Bang or when the Big Bang was at the point of Planck time when the Universe was only one ten-million-trillion-trillion-trillionth (10^{-43}) of a second old? Along with Albert Einstein and his General Theory of Relativity, it was Max Planck who started us on the journey through the quantum realm toward an understanding of the earliest instants of the Big Bang Universe.

Max Planck and the Early Universe

The German physicist Max Planck was formulating early quantum theory back in 1899, when gaslights lit the Berlin streets at night and horse-drawn carriages took people place to place. With his work on radiation and wavelength, Planck built a new house of physics for the twentieth century. The house of classical physics had been outgrown. Little did Planck realize that his early quantum-theory formulas provided glimpses into the physics of the middle- and late-twentieth century, into the world of supercomputers and the new cosmology of the Big Bang, where scientists and theorists would be attempting to understand what was happening on the subatomic level when the Universe was *much less* than a trillionth of a second old.

Planck discovered that radiating bodies emit their energy in discrete units, which he called quanta, not in a continuous flow. A quantum is therefore the smallest amount of

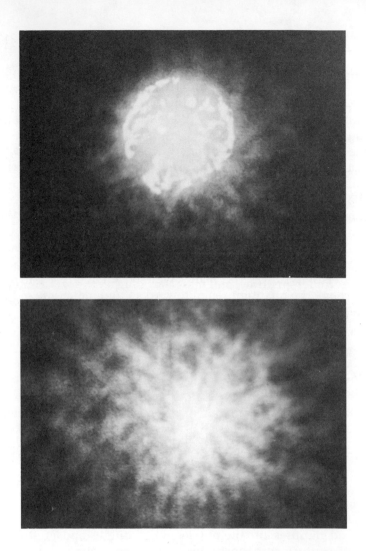

Artist's rendering of the Big Bang. When the Big Bang was less than one trillionth of a second old, our entire Universe was smaller than a grain of sand, a needle's point, or even the nucleus of one of your red blood cells! From the film *The Universe, Courtesy NASA.*

energy that can be radiated or absorbed by matter at a particular frequency. He formulated what is now called Planck's constant (or law), which states that each quantum of radiated energy (photon) has a certain wavelength, and the amount of energy in the photon is inversely proportional to its wavelength. His formula was able to describe the amount of radiation at each wavelength coming each second from 1 square centimeter of a so-called black body (an ideal scientific construct that absorbs or emits radiation of all wavelengths), which emits radiation only as a function of its temperature.

During Planck's formulation of early quantum theory, he made some curious observations from his equations of the micro world. He stated that there were natural or standard units for length, time, and mass that allowed the equations of physics to take particularly simple forms. All these units were inconceivably small. The unit for mass was perhaps the easiest to comprehend—about the size of a small grain of dust. But the time and length units were far, far smaller than anything that could have meaning in terms of the physics of the turn of the century.* The Planck unit of length was less than billionths of trillionths of trillionths of an inch—so much smaller than the diameter of an atom that the same scale proportion could be made between the diameter of an atom and a distance of several light-years to faraway stars. And then there was Planck's unit for time, 10^{-43} second. Planck time is such an infinitesimal instant that it has the same proportion to the time it would take light to travel the distance of the thickness of a thin sheet of paper (about 1/360 of an inch, 0.07 millimeter) as this micro light-time has to the estimated age of the Universe—about 18 billion years! This Planck time, beyond which Einstein's General Theory of Relativity cannot predict conditions, is usually considered to be the beginning time of the Big Bang, the birth time of our Universe. These are the micro realms where cosmologists

---

* Planck's actual values: mass = 2.9×10^{-5} gram; length = 1.61×10^{-33} centimeter; and time = 5.36×10^{-44} second.

and quantum and high-energy physicists spend their working lives looking for the ultimate answers of the Universe. And some amazing theories have come out of this work in recent years, work that has as its foundation those micro values that Planck formulated way back in 1899 in the city of Berlin.

Foamlike Space-Time

Today's theoretical physicists such as Stephen Hawking and John Wheeler have even attempted to understand what happened before the Big Bang, before Planck time. One such theory states that before the Big Bang, before the birth of our Universe, time and space were very different from the smooth, continuously flowing media of our experience. Because there was nothing with which to measure distances or intervals of time, we could say that everything was happening all at once, and in the same place. It is the Planck units that describe what was happening.

To understand space and time before the Big Bang, think of a large pile of whipped cream. From a distance, even up close, the cream looks smooth, uniform, and continuous. But if we examine it with a microscope, tiny bubbles are seen within it, all forming and bursting, then forming anew.

In a way, this is what space and time were like. New theory has it that, at any moment, any point in space could spontaneously become a microscopic black hole, with a mass given by Planck's value unit for mass, equal to a small grain of dust. That black hole would have a radius given by Planck's extremely small value for length. But the black hole would not live long; it would rapidly evaporate back into the space from which it formed, and it would do this in Planck's time.

Planck's quantum length or distance (trillions of times less than a trillionth of an inch) has even more significance. Down to that range of distance, space was smooth and even. But at even shorter lengths, it ceased to have three dimensions. Space had, instead, ten dimensions. The others were rolled up, curled up within Planck's distance.

This rolling or curling might best be understood by imagining a garden hose. A hose is a three-dimensional object. But two of its dimensions—its width and height—are rolled up within a radius of a centimeter or so. What remains is its length, the one remaining dimension. Somewhat similarly, the seven extra dimensions of space are curled up inside the Planck distance, leaving the three common dimensions that we see and measure.

Prior to the Big Bang, all that was happening in space and time took place within lengths and times given by the Planck numbers. At that minute scale, space and time were violently active things, continually casting up mini black holes, dissolving them, curling away into seven extra dimensions, reconnecting and forming new black holes. This is called the foamlike structure of space-time.

A Single Force

The play of sunlight on a lawn, the cascade of a waterfall, the eruption of lava in a volcano, and the soft green glow of a clock's hands at night—each of these in turn represents one of the four basic forces of nature. The light on the lawn comes from electromagnetism. The waterfall represents gravity. The lava comes from nuclear reactions deep within the core of the Earth, which are governed by the "strong force," the force that holds atomic nuclei together. And the clock's soft glow comes from the "weak force," which controls radioactivity, the source of the glow's energy.

But before the Universe began, theory tells us, there were not four forces, but, rather, only a single force. We call it the unified force. The unified force acted on the mini black holes, bringing them into existence from within the foamlike structure.

Scientists have begun to work with the unification of forces within our most powerful high-energy accelerators. In 1983 Carlo Rubbia and Simon Van der Meer demonstrated the unification of the weak and electromagnetic forces by creating the particles known as the W and the Z, which arise within this unification. The next level of unification would bring in the strong force. Theories that attempt to describe these three forces in their high-energy, unified state are known as Grand Unified Theories (abbreviated to GUTs). But to create their particles would take a trillion times more energy than it took to form the W and Z particles. To go all the way to a full Unified Field Theory, which would bring in gravity as well, the fourth force, it would take 100,000 times more energy still. These theories are known as SuperGUTs.

Yet, before the Universe began, such inconceivable energies freely existed and created the mini black holes. Our best labs fall short of the necessary energy by a factor of 100,000 trillion. But amid the enormous energies of the pre-Universe, the mini black holes arose spontaneously, simply because the needed energy was freely available.

The Lightweight Universe

How could mini black holes arise out of nothing? There is a law that says particles can arise this way as long as they disappear rapidly. A comparison can be made between this and bank embezzlement. A bank clerk can "borrow" a small sum for a reasonably long time, without the risk of getting caught. But if he steals a large sum, he must put it back quickly, because it will soon be noticed and missed.

The way this works in physics is that a mini black hole, having the infinitesimal Planck mass, can live no longer than the Planck time before it must return to the void. Lighter particles, arising out of nothing, can live for longer times, and a particle of zero mass can live forever. The Universe, new theory tells us, was created out of the void, and if it is not to live forever, its life span approaches the concept of eternity. But how can the entire Universe have zero mass?

Within the Universe as we see it, there are matter and energy. These add up to the equivalent of a very large mass. But there is also gravitational attraction. This carries a very large negative energy, which is just another form of mass, a way of expressing negative mass. The sum of the two, the Universe's gravity together with its ordinary matter and energy, appears to be extremely close to zero. This means that our Universe could have been created out of nothing, with a total mass of zero. If this is true, the Universe can live forever.

Stephen Hawking has recently worked out a theory of this type to explain the origin of the Universe. In his theory, the Universe could have formed in any size, but the most likely size for it was to be infinite in extent. Paradoxically, it not only is larger than anything we can name, it also is less dense than anything science has ever measured.

Birth of the Big Bang

The Big Bang started with the simultaneous creation of time, space, and gravity. Gravity arose from a "freezing out" of the unified force. Just as water freezes out from cooling steam, so gravity separated out, in a somewhat similar fashion. The other three forces—strong, weak, and electromagnetic—remained unified. But now, with gravity in existence, there arose the opportunity for standards of comparison against which events could have well-defined separation in time and space. That is how they came into existence.

During the first 10^{-35} second (one 100-billion-trillion-trillionth of a second), the three forces remained unified. The Universe was unimaginably hot, at 1,000 trillion trillion degrees Kelvin, or 10^{27} degrees. At such temperatures, the unification maintained itself naturally, somewhat as water remains liquid at appropriate temperatures. Usually water freezes into ice at 32 degrees Fahrenheit. But if we proceed with care the water can be chilled well below this temperature and still remain liquid. Then, all of a sudden, *part* of this "supercooled water" turns to ice. As it does this, heat is released, and the heat warms the supercooled unfrozen water back to 32 degrees Fahrenheit.

Theory tells us that just this type of supercooling appears to have taken place during the Universe's earliest instants. With the Universe expanding in the early Big Bang, at an age of less than one 100-billion-trillion-trillionth (10^{-35}) of a second, its temperature dropped below the 1,000-trillion-trillion-degree mark. This should have caused the electroweak force—the still-unified electromagnetic and weak combined force—to separate out from the strong force. But the Universe was cooling so rapidly that this did not happen immediately. Instead, the three forces persisted in their unified state, in what amounted to a supercooling of these forces. This state of the Universe, with the three forces still unified, is called the "false vacuum" by the new cosmologists. From it, very quickly in the micro-time dimension, emerged the Universe of the Big Bang.

The Inflationary Universe

At the mind-boggling age of 10^{-35} second (one 100-billion-trillion-trillionth of a second), the entire Universe we observe today could have fit into a region far smaller than the Planck distance. This region, in turn, was only a small part of a much larger region of the Universe that was still extremely small on the human scale—10^{-25} centimeter (one 10-trillion-trillionth of a centimeter) across. This region was connected into a single whole because light could travel across it and influence events at various locations. Beyond this connected region were infinitely many other such regions, which filled the infinite Universe but could not influence our connected region, or make their presence known within it.

Our connected region, containing the microcosmic part that would eventually become our observable Universe, was made up of a false vacuum. Within its "supercooled" state, that false vacuum had an enormously excessive energy—far beyond what it would have had if the strong force and the electroweak force had separated out. That excess energy drove our connected region into an immensely rapid expansion. In about one 100-million-trillion-trillionth (10^{-32}) of a second, the connected region blew up from its incredibly microcosmic size into a size of over 1 billion light-years—equal to a large portion of today's observed Universe. The part that would become our observed Universe also inflated.

It went from much smaller than the Planck distance to the size of a grapefruit—all within 10^{-32} second, or one 100-million-trillion-trillionth of a second.

During this inflation, this super-rapid expansion, the three forces remained unified and supercooled. But at the end of this inflationary period, after the 10^{-32} second, they finally separated out. Now the electroweak force was at last distinct and different from the strong force.

This separation released an immense burst of energy throughout the very early Universe. This was the excess energy that had driven the expansion. This energy reheated the Universe, which had been supercooled to "only" 10 billion trillion (10^{22}) degrees, back to 1,000 trillion trillion (10^{27}) degrees. This energy was now available to create the fundamental particles, the quarks, from which the atoms and matter of the Universe would eventually form.

The energy arose at the expense of gravitational energy within the Universe, which took on a large and negative value as the energy released from the false vacuum took on an equally large and positive value. As Alan Guth, the originator of this theory, puts it: "The universe may be the ultimate free lunch." That is how he describes the creation of matter out of nothing, and while inflation may be bad news in economics, it is very good news for cosmology. Alan Guth's theories have taken us farther than ever before toward understanding the origin of the Big Bang.

Creating Matter

With the strong and the electroweak forces now well separated, the Universe ceased to be supercooled and could settle down to a normal state of expansion. We call it the Big Bang. The energy of the false vacuum then created immense numbers of quarks and antiquarks. These amounted to matter and antimatter, which filled the Universe with 10 billion times more matter than it would eventually hold.

Through the interactions between quarks, there was a slight excess—1 part in 10 billion—of quarks over antiquarks.

For every 10 billion antiquarks, there were 10 billion and 1 quarks. The two types represented matter and antimatter. Soon they annihilated and converted themselves back into energy. But the small excess of quarks lived on, eventually to form galaxies, stars, planets, and people.

If this excess had not existed—if the quarks and antiquarks had been evenly balanced in numbers—then the Universe would have filled with energy, but there would have been no matter as we know it. The reason we exist, the reason this book is here for you to read, is that subtle features of the physics of quarks in the first 10^{-30} second (one million-trillion-trillionth) of a second, produced this slight excess of quarks over antiquarks.

From Quarks to Atoms

After the time of inflation, until the Universe was about a trillionth of a second old, it consisted of an extremely hot and dense "soup" of quarks and antiquarks, positrons and electrons, photons, and various types of neutrinos. During this trillionth of a second, the Universe expanded and cooled a trillionfold. Its temperature dropped from 1,000 trillion trillion (10^{27}) degrees to 1,000 trillion (10^{15}) degrees. At this point, the electroweak force separated out into the electromagnetic and weak forces, after which they were no longer unified: they became separate and distinct.

The dense "soup" persisted for another millionth of a second, as the Universe cooled to 1 trillion degrees. At this point in time and space, the Universe was cool enough for the quarks to come together to make protons and neutrons, as well as other particles. By the time the Universe was a second old, this process had been completed, filling the Universe with protons and neutrons.

These particles could now begin to take part in nuclear reactions. During the next three minutes, the protons and neutrons formed atomic nuclei, and their reactions quickly turned one quarter of the mass of the Universe into helium. Most of the rest was hydrogen. We can observe the helium today within the depths of space. It testifies to the extreme conditions of this early phase of the Universe—far hotter and denser than in a hydrogen bomb or in the center of a star.

In the world of nuclear reactions, it is no easy thing to "cook" hydrogen into helium. This reaction is the basis for our Sun's energy, but it takes billions of years for this to occur in the Sun. By contrast, in the early Universe a full one quarter of the hydrogen was "cooked" in a mere three minutes. The reason the Universe could do this was that it had extremely high temperature and density. Its temperature was a billion degrees—seventy times hotter than the Sun's center. Its density was ten times greater than that of water, making it as dense as lead.

Following the creation of the atomic nuclei, nothing much happened for some 700,000 years. The Universe continued to cool and expand, but it was still too hot to form atoms. Electrons and nuclei existed side by side. The Universe finally cooled down to only a few thousand degrees. When this occurred, the electrons could attach to the nuclei, creating the atoms we see today. It would be these atoms that would form the galaxies and stars. And a remnant of the formation of atoms is visible today—the 2.7-degree background radiation, the original evidence for the Big Bang, predicted by George Gamow in 1948 and discovered by Arno Penzias and Robert Wilson in 1965. This radiation, from the time when the first atoms were formed in the cooling cosmos, was created when the Universe was less than 1 million years old.

Fifty Decimal Places

Just as the mass of an individual star determines its life cycle and the way it will eventually die, so too does the mass of the Universe determine its ultimate fate. Cosmologists usually describe three possible types of Universe, and the choice depends on whether the density of the Universe is subcritical, supercritical, or critical. A subcritically dense Universe will expand forever; it corresponds to a rocket that leaves the Earth with a speed greater than escape velocity. A supercritically dense Universe will expand for some billions of years but then collapse, somewhat like a rocket that rises for a while but then falls back to Earth. The critically dense Universe is like a rocket fired with the precise escape velocity. It will expand forever, but the rate of expansion, although it never stops, grows slower and slower over extremely distant time.

The advent of the inflationary scenario to describe the Universe during its first 10^{-32} second (one 100-million-trillion-trillionth of a second) gives cosmologists an excellent reason to favor the critically dense Universe today. During that phase of expansion, the Universe may well have inflated 10^{50}-fold (100-trillion-trillion-trillion-trillion-fold) or more. At the beginning of the inflation, the Universe may have been supercritical or subcritical. But the difference between its true density and the critical density would have been greatly reduced during the inflation. Indeed, this difference would have shrunk by the same factor: 10^{50} or more.

How close was the density to the critical value during the Big Bang? Alan Guth, inventor of the inflationary scenario of the early Universe, declares that it was so close, it was as if someone were to balance a pencil on its point and still have it balancing upright a billion years later. With the Universe being critically dense to an accuracy of fifty decimal places, today's cosmologists frequently declare that its density was exactly critical—to as many decimal places as one would wish. If correct, this means that the Universe will expand at a steadily diminishing rate. Eventually this rate will be extremely slow. A day will come when galaxies, now flying away from us at half the speed of light, will slow to the speed of 1 foot (0.3 meter) every billion years!

The Missing Mass

How much mass does modern astronomy detect in the Universe? This is one of the most outstanding problems in astronomy today. Where is the mass that brings the matter of the Universe up to the critical value? Does it exist at all? Stars and galaxies—the matter that glows in the dark—total only a few percent of the needed mass. From analyses of the motions of galaxies, it becomes apparent that there is a great deal of missing mass, which is not observed with present astronomical techniques. But the gravity of the mass is known, because it makes galaxies move more rapidly than if the mass were absent. This is how astronomers know it is there.

Even so, this detectable part of the missing mass amounts to only one sixth of what is needed for the critical density. The deficiency becomes less serious as astronomers look out upon more and more distant realms. As they advance from single galaxies to rich clusters of galaxies, and then on to the immense assemblages known as superclusters, they discover a trend: effects of gravity, which can be observed, show more and more of the missing mass. According to some estimates, the amount of mass that can thus be accounted for is at least several tenths of that needed for the critical density of the Universe.

It would seem that astronomers still have a good way to go. It is possible that the Universe has a density less than critical, which would allow it to expand forever at high speed. If this is so, the theoretical scenario of the inflationary Universe runs into serious problems. But the theory works well by solving many problems that were associated with the original Big Bang model of the Universe. The inflationary theory would have the Universe near critical density, accurate to fifty decimal places, but not *exactly* at critical density. The difference would grow with time, until it would show up in today's Universe as a density just a little less than critical. But this is hard to believe. Cosmologists see no easy way to have critical density out to fifty decimal places without the Universe being exactly critical.

Moreover, the idea of creating the Universe out of nothing also brings the conclusion that the Universe must be exactly of critical density. This way, its matter and energy exactly balance its gravitational energy, so that they sum to zero. If the Universe were at less than critical density, there would be an imbalance, and the Universe could not have been created out of nothing—which is the most straightforward way to understand where it did come from.

Today's best astronomical observations do not yet tell the whole story. There is evidently more mass out there than can yet be accounted for—some is still missing. And since this is at least half the mass of our Universe, and probably 90 percent or more, we can say that astronomers have yet to discover most of the Universe; so far they have found only a small part.

Adding Up the Missing Mass

An army of astronomers are laboriously searching for the missing mass—hard-to-detect matter such as thin intergalactic gas, Jupiter-sized planets, massive black holes, dark galaxies, and the ever-elusive elementary particles, neutrinos. Whatever and wherever the missing mass is, it is certainly no trifling matter. It equals as much as 1 trillion of our Milky Way galaxies. That could amount to more mass than 100 billion trillion stars.

The Hubble Space Telescope will probe the depths of space and time. It will detect and gather light from distant galaxies and quasars that have never been seen before. It has the ability to observe objects that are fifty times fainter than any Earth-based telescope can detect, and it can peer seven times farther into space than previous equipment, which means that it will observe a volume of space that is 350 times larger than what astronomy could in the past. The Hubble Space Telescope is 1 billion times more sensitive to light than the human eye. Its state-of-the-art equipment will discover regions of the Universe that have heretofore been hidden in the depths of space and time. In its first few years of operation, it may find much of the missing mass, and by the time it ends its operational life, early in the twenty-first century, we may finally know if the Universe is an opened or closed case.

The Hubble Space Telescope will help to find the missing mass of the Universe and may eventually determine its far-future fate. Will it all end with a whimper or a bang? *Courtesy Perkin-Elmer Corporation.*

What Is the Missing Mass?

There are many ideas and theories that attempt to tell us what form the missing mass might take. Here are a few of them.

Dark Galaxies. One of the simplest of the theories is that of Nicholas Kaiser, at Cambridge University. He holds that most of the mass in the Universe takes the form of dark galaxies, which are too tenuous to produce stars that astronomers can detect. Such galaxies would cool to the temperature of intergalactic space, 2.7 degrees above absolute zero, and it would be extremely difficult to see them.

In Kaiser's view, galaxies form with a range of densities. The range is such that most of them are too tenuous to produce stars. Only a few are made of the denser stuff, which creates the stars we can see. So while we look out at the galaxies and think we see them all, like the cities lit up at night, in fact most of them would be like cities blacked out, whose presence would never be suspected.

The Fateful Neutrino. Neutrinos are subatomic particles that are extremely difficult to detect and are theoretically believed to occur when a neutron ejects an electron, resulting in a proton. They were always believed to have no mass and to travel at the speed of light. Recent evidence may indicate, however, that neutrinos actually oscillate between three states, constantly changing hats.

If neutrinos do indeed oscillate, they must have mass— estimated at between 16 and 40 electron volts, which is about thirteen thousand times less than the mass of an electron, until now considered the lightest particle with mass. And if neutrinos prove out to have mass, then they are the dominant material of the Universe—about 10,000 neutrinos for every 6 cubic inches (100 cubic centimeters) of the Universe—and may provide all the missing mass that astronomers have been seeking for decades, mass that could provide enough gravity eventually to reverse the expansion of the Universe.

With mass, neutrinos could not travel at the speed of light, and massive objects such as galaxies could capture them. This could mean that immense massive neutrino clouds are pervading space, undetected by astronomers. If so, the Universe would contain enough mass to be closed and would ultimately collapse.

WIMPs. Another class of theories hold that there are unusual particles filling the Universe, particles that carry mass but also elude detection. One of the more intriguing of these particles is called the WIMP, Weakly Interacting Massive Particle. According to the physicist John Faulkner, WIMPs that fill the Universe do more than produce the missing mass; they also solve an important problem involving our Sun's energy.

For over fifteen years, the physicist Raymond Davies has

been measuring the flow of neutrinos from the solar core. These neutrinos serve as a probe of conditions at the Sun's core. There are well-established theories to predict how many neutrinos should be seen, but Davies has consistently found only one third as many as are expected. This could be explained if the solar core is cooler than expected. But there is no easy way to see how this could be, for under the standard theory, a cooler core should lead to a Sun that is dimmer than it actually is.

The WIMPs appear to solve this problem. These particles, according to the theory, can carry off heat from the Sun's core to the surrounding regions. This allows the core to be cooler, the neutrino flow to be less, and the Sun's brightness to be as intense as we actually observe it. If these ideas are correct, the WIMP solves two problems at once, problems that no one had ever before thought were related. There was no clue that the missing solar neutrinos might be explained as being related to the missing mass of the Universe.

At present, these are only ideas and theories. It will take a lot more work before astronomers know the true nature of the missing mass. One thing is, however, already clear: it will take a form that is quite unfamiliar. Since the time of Copernicus, we have learned that humankind is not at the center of the Solar System and not at the center of the Galaxy. There is nothing unique or special about the Sun or the Milky Way. But now we are coming to understand that our bodies and our world are not even made up of the form of matter that is predominant in the Universe.

The Big Squeeze and Crunch

If the Universe has enough mass, if it is found to be supercritically dense, then it will eventually halt its expansion and begin to collapse. It would be a closed, finite Universe. Although this scenario is out of favor with cosmologists who believe that the inflationary Big Bang is the best theory, it still is a possibility. Assuming that the mass of the Universe is large enough to cause a future collapse, what would happen?

Perhaps 50 billion years from now, the Universe would begin its collapse and compression. Galaxies would move toward one another, at first slowly and then with ever-increasing velocity. The temperature of the Universe would begin to rise because of the compressed radiation. About 50 billion years after the start of the contraction, the Universe would be the same size as it is today. Billions of years later still, when the Universe contracts to one hundredth its present size, the invisible cosmic microwave radiation, at longer wavelengths than light, would become visible and, if Earth still exists in some form, the dark night sky would glow deep red and become as warm as our present daytime sky—about 27 degrees Celsius, or 80.6 degrees Fahrenheit. Another 100 million years or so would find the Universe about one thousandth its present size, and the Earth's sky would be blindingly bright.

As the universal compression continues, galaxies would collide, their immense gravitational systems tugging and twisting one another. Their stars and interstellar gas clouds would collide also. Soon all planets and stars would dissolve in the cosmic caldron. Heat and density would first break up all the complex molecules, leaving only hydrogen and helium. As in the beginning, the Universe would become an extremely dense and hot soup of matter. The cosmic Big Squeeze, space-time counterpart to the Big Bang, would take the Universe back to the unknown realm that lies behind the Planck doors of quantum units, perhaps to the unknown realm of singularity—the ultimate black hole. Such a contracting Universe, like an infinitely expanding one, may become, finally and absolutely, nothing at all.

A Bouncing Universe?

Again putting aside the inflationary Big Bang model of the Universe for the moment, let us again assume that the

Universe has a supercritical mass and will collapse. Once the Universe experiences the Big Squeeze and rushes toward its fiery destiny with quantum realities behind the Planck wall, where both time and theory must have a stop, what lies beyond? No one knows and only few will speculate.

One alternative ending to this possible collapsing Universe that ends with the Great Question Mark is the so-called oscillating (or bouncing) Universe, which holds unchallenged appeal for the romantics among us. In this model, a new Big Bang occurs at some point before Planck's quantum units of mass, length, and time come into play, and another expanding Universe begins. The cycle repeats itself and, like the phoenix, the Universe is born again from its own ashes. One estimate for the period of such an expansion-contraction cycle, based on many assumptions, is 150 billion years—about ten times the present age of the Universe.

How the Universe could bounce back from the Big Squeeze and cataclysmic implosion is not known and remains one of the many mysteries. But speculative theory suggests that there may be created new elementary particles of different mass and charge and a completely new set of laws for physics. The lifetimes of new universes would vary—some may be longer than 80 billion years (a length calculated for the present Universe if it should in reality match the bouncing model), and some may last only a few million years. If future universes were such brief bounces, expanding for only a few million years, they would also be extremely small—too brief and too small for galaxy and star formation; indeed, too brief and small for that long-odds marvel called life.

A Forever Open Universe?

When pressed for an opinion on how the Universe will end, the physicist Stephen Hawking, who has been called Einstein's equal by some, claims that no one knows. But if he had to choose a cosmological model, he would pick the one that predicts an expanding Universe with just enough energy to avoid collapse—one that is on the borderline between expansion and collapse. This is the critically dense model of the Universe, the one that expands forever but constantly slows down. It is the future Universe predicted by the inflationary model of the Big Bang described earlier in this chapter.

Assuming such an open Universe, what will happen in the far cosmic future, the distant future when immense vistas of time are so enormous that 1 trillion years (1,000 billion years), more than fifty-five times the estimated age of our Universe today (about 18 billion years), will be only an instant in this almost eternal future?

Over trillions of future years, the galaxies will use up the masses of hydrogen needed for new star birth, and new stars will become extremely rare. There will be mostly dying stars, red and brown dwarfs, and there will be millions of darkening galaxies. But forms of life still could survive in this distant future. Great structures could be erected around the dying stars to capture every photon of the fading light. Such structures are known as Dyson spheres, named after the Princeton physicist Freeman Dyson, who has speculated about advanced civilizations dismantling planets to build such star-surrounding spheres.

The galaxies will fly farther and farther away from one another in the expanding, ever-slowing Universe. If humankind or its evolutionary lineage survives to this far future, somehow getting a longer life out of the dying Sun or finding a new home star, historic photos or images of other galaxies would be priceless, since they would no longer be visible from Earth and our Milky Way—or from any other galaxy in the Universe. Most of the Universe would have literally disappeared for any viewer in any galaxy.

Our Milky Way Galaxy will share the fate of all other galaxies. Its tens of billions of stars will eventually burn out, including our yellow dwarf Sun, their nuclear fuels exhausted, never to radiate light again. A few old red stars will still dimly burn, but most of the Galaxy will be dead matter— dead neutron and white-dwarf stars, and black holes. Then the Galaxy will lose its spiral structure, and its central core will become even more dense. The immense black hole in its center will become even larger. What was once the planet Earth might make its way to the Galaxy's center. Flying through space at nearly the speed of light as it approaches, it might be swallowed whole by the great black hole and vanish forever from our Universe. Nothing, not even light, could escape from this monstrous gravitational vortex.

Trillions of more years into the future Universe and there will be billions of great black holes where luminous galaxies once existed. A thin, diffuse gas will permeate space, and it is there where new, plasma forms of "life" could exist.

Freeman Dyson envisions the possibilities of such new life forms in the distant future of the Universe. Such ionized plasma, Dyson speculates, is "the kind of stuff that can behave in an enormously complicated fashion, and can therefore carry a great deal of information, like DNA. It has at least the potential for organizing itself in interesting ways." And as the temperature of the Universe falls, Dyson adds, these plasma life forms can retain their structures "by spreading over longer distances and living more slowly." Even in the freezing night of the future Universe, Dyson believes that "life will have just enormous opportunities for experimenting, trying out different forms of existence." And such future life forms could tap the black-hole whirlpools for energy, because there will be a great abundance of black holes of all sizes—gravitational graveyards for spent matter.

A variety of life forms could probably survive into the future Universe for a time that is equal to 20 to 30 billion times the present age of the Universe. After that, however, all forms of matter that we know in today's Universe will have disappeared. The subatomic decay of protons and neutrons will reign in the cosmic realm; the nuclei of atoms will break down. Over greater periods of future time, proton decay will turn all atoms into energy. Only positrons (the antimatter of electrons) and electrons will remain. If they are too close to one another, they will vanish in a burst of gamma rays. If positrons and electrons orbit one another at a distance (and there will be immensities of distance in the ever-expanding Universe), they will form an atom of positronium. It is positronium that will be the only material available for the possibility of plasma-type life in this incomprehensibly distant time. These positronium atoms will be the last atoms of the Universe.

In this speculative scenario of an ever-expanding Universe, the great black holes that once were galaxies will find one another in the vastness, and combine. The small black holes will evaporate over the trillions of years, and the large, galactic black holes will last into the extremely far future, before they, too, disappear. They will share this dark, frozen, immensely expanded Universe with positronium and photons. The observable Universe of today will have expanded 10^{67} times in volume, which has utterly no human meaning because it would be 10 million trillion trillion trillion trillion trillion times the volume of today's Universe. The positrons and electrons will be moving only a few feet, a meter, every 100 million years, and when they form atoms of positronium, each atom will be 1 billion times larger than the entire visible Universe of today!

This all sounds absurd, absolutely impossible. But is this any more difficult to comprehend than other aspects of the inflationary Big Bang Universe, which describes the Universe as having come forth from nothing, a Universe that might have a mass of exactly 0?

Where is the meaning in all this? A frozen, black Universe that slowly grows larger and larger and in the far distant future contains only one, strange type of atom, each component of which is more than 1 billion times larger than today's observable Universe! What can a person do with this? Be grateful that today's Universe allows us to exist at all? Yes. These are good times for life in the Universe. You may find this hard to believe, but it could be a lot, lot worse. There could be no life anywhere in the Universe. But *we* exist. We wonder. We begin to fly between the planets and moons that orbit our Sun. But even in our Solar System, which is benign because it includes the planet Earth, there is no where else humankind can survive without expensive and challenging adaptations; we have to carry little Earths along with us. Could it be that we've had more than our share of cosmic luck?

If science ever knows for certain the fate of the Universe, what will this tell us? It will tell us the ultimate fate of the atoms that now make up our living bodies and brains, the same atoms that allow us to exist and struggle to give meaning to the Universe and to our brief lives.

INDEX

ABOUT THE AUTHOR

Neil McAleer was born in 1942, in Richmond, Virginia, and now lives in New Cumberland, Pennsylvania. He holds a bachelor's degree from the University of New Mexico and a master's degree in English literature from Southern Illinois University. Mr. McAleer is a member of the Authors Guild and is listed in *Contemporary Authors.*

From 1974 to 1979 he was editorial director of a Pennsylvania publishing house, where he created a successful list of science books including the best-selling *Colonies in Space* and established other new publishing directions with such books as *The Beatles Forever.*

His own work includes both fiction and nonfiction. *Earthlove,* a fantasy novel, was his first published book, followed by *The Cosmic Mind-Boggling Book, The Body Almanac,* and *The Omni Space Almanac.*